God of Justice

THE IJM INSTITUTE *Global Church Curriculum*

Abraham George
& Nikki A. Toyama-Szeto

IVP Connect

An imprint of InterVarsity Press
Downers Grove, Illinois

InterVarsity Press
P.O. Box 1400, Downers Grove, IL 60515-1426
ivpress.com
email@ivpress.com

InterVarsity Press® is the book-publishing division of InterVarsity Christian Fellowship/USA®, a movement of students and faculty active on campus at hundreds of universities, colleges and schools of nursing in the United States of America, and a member movement of the International Fellowship of Evangelical Students. For information about local and regional activities, visit intervarsity.org.

All Scripture quotations, unless otherwise indicated, are taken from THE HOLY BIBLE, NEW INTERNATIONAL VERSION®, NIV® Copyright © 1973, 1978, 1984, 2011 by Biblica, Inc.™ Used by permission. All rights reserved worldwide.

While any stories in this book are true, some names and identifying information may have been changed to protect the privacy of individuals.

Cover design: Cindy Kiple
Interior design: Beth McGill
Images: Cover and interior photographs ©2015 International Justice Mission

ISBN 978-0-8308-1028-4 (print)
ISBN 978-0-8308-9865-7 (digital)

Printed in the United States of America ∞

Library of Congress Cataloging-in-Publication Data
A catalog record for this book is available from the Library of Congress.

P	24	23	22	21	20	19	18	17	16	15	14	13	12	11	10	9	8	7	6	5	4	3	2	1
Y	36	35	34	33	32	31	30	29	28	27	26	25	24	23	22	21	20	19	18	17	16	15		

"I love everything about this guide—the stories, the questions, the Scriptures, the prayers, the insights into personal and systemic issues that perpetuate injustice all over the world. Since God is a God of justice, this study will lead you deeper into the heart of God. And there is no one better than the staff of IJM to help you get there!"

Ruth Haley Barton, founder, Transforming Center, author of *Strengthening the Soul of Your Leadership*

"This is a wonderful resource for the church! It's a great Bible study overviewing God's heart for justice and the role it plays in the overarching biblical story. May more churches gain God's heart for the vulnerable and oppressed through this study."

Eddie Byun, author of *Justice Awakening*

"Combining years of frontline experience with deep biblical reflection, *God of Justice* is an essential resource. Toyama-Szeto and George provide the global church with the tools to engage with issues of shalom and human dignity in a world marred by violence."

Gary A. Haugen, president, International Justice Mission

Contents

Introduction

While pointing out the reason God was not responding to the prayer and fasting of the people, the prophet Isaiah also names the very essence of what God really requires:

> Is not this the kind of fasting I have chosen:
> to loose the chains of injustice
>   and untie the cords of the yoke,
> to set the oppressed free
>   and break every yoke?
> Is it not to share your food with the hungry
>   and to provide the poor wanderer with shelter—
> when you see the naked, to clothe them,
>   and not to turn away from your own flesh and blood? (Isaiah 58:6-7)

In this passage, the prophet highlights the religious practice of fasting and redefines it in rather non-religious terms. It is not about the foods one can eat but rather the actions taken on behalf of and in connection with the marginalized. All of Isaiah 58 shows a connection between worship of God and acts of justice on behalf of the most vulnerable. The nation of Israel is challenged to see that their relationship with others, particularly those who have been cast aside in their community, affects their relationship with God.

This is indeed the mandate that we, as Christ-followers, have been given: to loose the chains of injustice, to untie the yoke, to set the oppressed free, to break every yoke, to share food, to provide shelter, to clothe the naked and not turn from our own flesh and blood! This is what God requires from his people. In the verses immediately preceding these, the prophet emphasizes that it is not even prayer and fasting or sackcloth and ashes God requires, but instead that we free those who are abused.

International Justice Mission (IJM), a human rights organization of Christian lawyers, social workers, investigators, advocates and educators, began its work in 1997. IJM began by taking seriously these words in Isaiah. And so the organization started to actively work to "loose the chains of injustice" for people caught in human trafficking, forced labor and other forms of violent injustice.

Since its beginning, IJM recognized that the church is a key part of God's work of justice. As IJM joined in a growing justice movement, we experienced some concern. Does this justice movement have the roots—the biblical grounding—to maintain a long-term, sustained engagement with these hard issues?

In 2010, IJM began helping churches in the Global South fight injustice in their communities. We quickly realized our mission was not going to be as easy as we had initially expected. In so many places, the church was far from embracing the prophet's definition of true religion.

As we worked in the Global South and elsewhere, we noticed a pattern for why churches did not easily embrace the prophet's description of true religion. First, there was either a significant lack of awareness of the injustices in their communities, or there was just a lack of awareness of adequate responses to these injustices. We thought this was best addressed through awareness-creating efforts. However, the second reason was a little more disconcerting to us. Just as in the passage from Isaiah, churches seemed to put more emphasis on certain religious observances, rituals and traditions instead of allowing "justice [to] roll on like a river" (Amos 5:24). Centuries of theological formulations and traditions had formed a thick cover on what was the essential kernel of God's mandate—at least in terms of the church's roles and responsibilities in this world—that needed to be peeled off. A spotlight needed to be shined on the core of God's heart.

This Bible study is our attempt to peel back those layers of traditions and skewed theologies and put the spotlight back on a core essential. It is also our attempt to deepen the roots of justice into its strong biblical foundation. We felt the need to journey with churches around the world and grapple with the ultimate divine plan to set things right—*shalom*.

But what is this shalom God intends, really? The prophet Isaiah again offers us a rather vivid picture of this vision of shalom—peace at last:

And he will delight in the fear of the LORD.

He will not judge by what he sees with his eyes,
    or decide by what he hears with his ears;
but with righteousness he will judge the needy,
    with justice he will give decisions for the poor of the earth.
He will strike the earth with the rod of his mouth;
    with the breath of his lips he will slay the wicked.
Righteousness will be his belt
    and faithfulness the sash around his waist.

The wolf will live with the lamb,
> the leopard will lie down with the goat,
the calf and the lion and the yearling together;
> and a little child will lead them.
The cow will feed with the bear,
> their young will lie down together,
> and the lion will eat straw like the ox.
The infant will play near the cobra's den,
> and the young child will put its hand into the viper's nest.
They will neither harm nor destroy
> on all my holy mountain,
for the earth will be filled with the knowledge of the LORD
> as the waters cover the sea. (Isaiah 11:3-9)

First articulated in the Old Testament poetic and prophetic literature and then expressed again in the New Testament, the idea of shalom places justice prominently at its core. Shalom is present when people live in harmony with God, and it is present when they live in harmony with nature. In addition, there is another key relationship that shalom encompasses. We also believe it is critically important to recognize that shalom is present when a person lives in perfect harmony with his/her fellow human beings. As people working with the victims of violent abuse around the world, this takes on special poignancy.

The prophet Isaiah introduces shalom in the previous passage with the following words, drawing a clear line of connection between God's plan for shalom and Jesus' mission in the world:

A shoot will come up from the stump of Jesse;
> from his roots a Branch will bear fruit.
The Spirit of the LORD will rest on him—
> the Spirit of wisdom and of understanding,
> the Spirit of counsel and of might,
> the Spirit of the knowledge and fear of the LORD. (Isaiah 11:1-2)

The picture Isaiah paints of shalom is directly connected to the mission of this branch from David's family—Jesus. It is impossible to miss the conclusion that shalom is not only God's cause but that we, as followers of Christ, must engage in the work of shalom.

Indeed, the full and final fulfillment of God's shalom in this world will be God's doing, just as the occasional glimpses we have of it today are his doing. Nevertheless, we cannot sit by idly and wait for God to bring it about. We are God's colaborers and it is our mission, just as it was of that branch from David's family, to work for freedom of the oppressed.

It is our hope in writing these Bible studies that the body of Christ around the world will be awakened to God's heart for the poor and the oppressed. It is our hope that the *missio Dei* (the mission of God) will bring freedom, and justice will become our mission as well. It is our hope that in poring over and grappling with the thoughts in these study sessions you will recognize without a doubt that God's heart for the poor and the oppressed is not just a peripheral concept, but that it forms the very heart and core of the gospel. It is what God desires.

Of course, shalom is bigger than justice, but to be sure, there will never be shalom without justice!

Suggestions for Study

Suggestions for Group Study

If you are preparing to lead a small group through this study, be encouraged that God is pleased with your desire to lead others closer to his heart for justice. This curriculum is designed to move people through observation, interpretation and application as they study the Scriptures and encounter the questions included. At the back of this curriculum you will find a **Facilitator's Guide**, which includes tips for preparation, leading a discussion and getting the most out of this small group experience. The guide also includes an "at a glance" look at each session, including key points and featured Scriptures. This will help you to see how the sessions are connected, and will assist you as you draw your group's attention to the main ideas and themes.

Suggestions for Individual Study

Consider this guidance as you prepare for your study.

- Before you begin each session, start with a time of prayer. Ask God to guide you into his truth and new understanding.

- Read the Scripture passage more than one time. Consider reading the passage out loud so you can hear the words as you speak them. As you read the Scripture, don't hesitate to mark the text, circling or underlining words that stand out to you, surprise you or cause you to question.

- Give appropriate time to each of the exercises. These were designed to aid in your understanding of the Scripture and to apply that understanding to your life. Accept the gift of time that this curriculum offers, and allow some space for you to connect your learning to what's happening every day in your life and in the world around you.

- Be open to what God will show you through this session. Consider how he might be prioritizing your inner transformation, and how he is leading you to change what you believe to be true about justice, how you value justice in your own life and how you can behave more justly on behalf of those who are in need of an advocate and a voice.

- Seek opportunities for you to live out what you've learned. Connect with friends, a small group, a church or a community service group. Move towards action.

We sincerely hope that this feels like a journey to you, one through which you can intentionally engage with the text and questions, finding at the end of your time a refreshing, enlivened and clearer perspective on the God of justice.

● **1**

God the Creator

"That is not fair!" toddlers scream. Each time I hear it, it amazes me that kids so young seem to have been born with an innate sense of fairness or justice. Usually it's defined as, "Am I getting what I want? Are you getting more than me?" And there is something about this passion that strikes me as something that must reflect God.

Yet our world dissolves absolutes and the definition of justice can become cloudy and confusing. One person's striving for justice tramples on another's freedom. We celebrate inclusivity of ideas, honor and respect different religions and cultures, and avoid judgment, hoping that makes everything good.

However, even as we become a society of many ideas and shy away from absolute truths, there are some things that we can and should agree on as a whole: it's not okay for someone to own another human being; the exploitation of children for their labor or their bodies is not permissible; violence is not acceptable. But where does this sense of the inherent worth of people come from?

This session will take us to a deeper look at some of God's original intentions and hopes for humanity.

As you begin this session, take a moment to think about what you hope to gain or understand through your learning about God and justice. Record some of your thoughts below.

What I know about justice:

What I would like to know or understand through this study:

What questions I'm hoping to have answered:

⌨ Read

Genesis 1:1-2, 11-12, 26-31; 2:1-3

[1]In the beginning God created the heavens and the earth. [2]Now the earth was formless and empty, darkness was over the surface of the deep, and the Spirit of God was hovering over the waters.

[11]Then God said, "Let the land produce vegetation; seed-bearing plants and trees on the land that bear fruit with seed in it, according to their various kinds." And it was so. [12]The land produced vegetation: plants bearing seed according to their kinds and trees bearing fruit with seed in it according to their kinds. And God saw that it was good.

[26]Then God said, "Let us make mankind in our image, in our likeness, so that they may rule over the fish in the sea and the birds in the sky, over the livestock and all the wild animals, and over all the creatures that move along the ground."

[27]So God created mankind in his own image,
    in the image of God he created them;
    male and female he created them.

[28]God blessed them and said to them, "Be fruitful and increase in number; fill the earth and subdue it. Rule over the fish in the sea and the birds in the sky and over every living creature that moves on the ground."
[29]Then God said, "I give you every seed-bearing plant on the face of the whole earth and every tree that has fruit with seed in it. They will be yours for food. [30]And to all the beasts of the earth and all the birds in the sky and all the creatures that move along the ground—everything that has the breath of life in it—I give every green plant for food." And it was so.
[31]God saw all that he had made, and it was very good. And there was evening, and there was morning—the sixth day.

2 Thus the heavens and the earth were completed in all their vast array.
    [2]By the seventh day God had finished the work he had been doing; so on the seventh day he rested from all his work. [3]Then God blessed the seventh day and made it holy, because on it he rested from all the work of creating that he had done.

Psalm 139:13-16

¹³For you created my inmost being;
    you knit me together in my mother's womb.
¹⁴I praise you because I am fearfully and wonderfully made;
    your works are wonderful,
    I know that full well.
¹⁵My frame was not hidden from you
    when I was made in the secret place,
    when I was woven together in the depths of the earth.
¹⁶Your eyes saw my unformed body;
    all the days ordained for me were written in your book
    before one of them came to be.

Reflect

■ **Question #1:** What characteristics of God do we see emerge from these two passages?

God's creation reveals his CHARACTER. These two passages introduce us to God the Creator. In Genesis, we see the power of God; he can create simply by speaking. In the psalm, we see the love and tenderness of God as he carefully crafts each individual. But more than anything, these passages teach us to view creation through God's eyes and to look for the goodness that he has poured into his creation. This session focuses on how the creation story reveals the dignity and value of each person. This will be explored through four key messages that come out of the scriptural story of creation.

■ **Question #2:** In Genesis, God says that his creation is "good." In what ways is this true when you look at the world around you?

God's creation reflects his GOODNESS. These two passages of Scripture reveal the act of creation as God's outpouring of his character in material form. We see God's goodness inhabiting all creation. In these verses, we see the unimaginable beauty and goodness of God: it takes a whole universe to reflect the many ways in which he is good.

It is important to notice that in the biblical account the creation of humanity is not a reaction to sin, nor is it the byproduct of war and violence as there was no violence or evil in God. In the Bible, we see that the true creation is the establishment of what is good by a God who is only good. This is seen in the continual refrain of Genesis 1: "And God saw that it was good." He did not create something that was both good and bad, but something that was altogether good. The creation story—as depicted in Genesis and the Psalms—teaches us about the character of God, that he is powerful and caring, mighty and tender.

■ **Question #3:** Look again at the Genesis passage. How does God respond to his creation in verse 31? What does this indicate about God's value of humanity?

Creation reveals the DIGNITY and VALUE of humanity. Both the passage from Genesis and from Psalms teach us about the *dignity* of humanity. As Psalm 139 teaches us, each of us is intricately woven by God. He creates each one of us carefully *in his own image* (Genesis 1:27). These truths give incredible value to each individual. When we look around us, we should be able to see each other as a reflection of God's goodness, as people individually and carefully crafted by our Maker. We are all deeply loved by God.

> God's creation teaches us that humans have *inherent* value that is not dependent on what we can do, say or achieve. We do not have to *do* anything for God to consider us good. Instead we *are* good because we are created by God.

God's creation teaches us that humans have *inherent* value that is not dependent on what we can do, say or achieve. In fact, in verse 31 God says that the creation of humans was "very good"—the very best of his creation. This means that as humans made in God's image, our value comes not from what we achieve, what family we are from or what other people think about us, but our value is woven into the fabric of our being. We do not have to *do* anything for God to consider us good. Instead, we *are* good because we are created by God. Creation teaches us that no person, no circumstance and no harsh word can diminish the value and dignity that God has woven into us.

■ **Question #4:** What do these passages teach us about people? When you look at the world around you, what are some ways that you see people treating each other that seem to contradict this truth?

God's mandate to humankind to procreate shows us that each new creation is a new source of goodness and is a good thing by itself. This should encourage us, when we look at ourselves and when we look at our neighbors, to see beings of the utmost beauty and value to God. These truths give us a remarkable foundation for treating others with immense dignity and respect. The knowledge that we are made in God's image and that God takes great care and delight over each detail of his creation will become vital later on when we look at why God hates injustice.

A church in London called Holy Trinity Brompton was putting on a huge worship event in the city to be held in the Royal Albert Hall, a huge and very beautiful concert hall. However, many more people signed up for the event than they were expecting. The organizers were left wondering how to seat these extra guests. Eventually, they decided to ask Buckingham Palace for permission to use the royal boxes. These are special, private balconies reserved for use by royals, heads of state and highly honored guests like Nelson Mandela and the president of the United States, so they were not sure what the answer would be. Buckingham Palace responded that yes, they may use the boxes, on the condition that they seat their most esteemed guests there. The organizers wrote back after the event to thank the Queen for her generosity. They wrote that yes, they indeed seated their most honored guests in the box, a group of homeless people who had wanted to attend the event.[1]

As Christians, we are called to look at people through the eyes of God, not of humanity. The creation story teaches us that we are all held in God's highest esteem, whether or not the world sees it that way. In God's eyes, the Queen of England and a homeless man are worthy of the same care and respect.

 Review

How might you explain what it means to be "made in God's image" to another person?

Children in Uganda sit in the entrance to their home, which was returned to them by IJM and local officials after a neighbor threatened to take their land.

❝❝ Respond

Exercise #1: How do others treat you? Your boss, your spouse, your friends, your neighbors? Are there things people do that affirm your role as one who is created in the image of God? Are there behaviors that discourage you from seeing yourself as a person created in the image of God? If so, what are some of the truths from God (from these passages or others) that you can reflect on? Use the chart below to answer these questions.

Person	Behaviors that affirm	Behaviors that discourage	God's truth

Exercise #2: Each and every person is made in the image of God. How has your role as an image bearer affected your actions, decisions and choices in the past twenty-four hours? How might it affect your decisions in the next twenty-four hours?

Complete the next chart. Who are the people that you encounter on a regular basis? Write their names in the first column. What can you do to affirm their role as people who reflect the Creator God? What actions do you want to reduce that might not be communicating their value as reflections of the Creator?

For example, it can be easy to take people for granted or ignore their personhood. We may begin to treat people as objects defined by their race, their gender, their job. After some reflection, I (Nikki) made a personal resolution that every time a waiter refilled my water, took my order or removed my dishes, I would say thank you and look him or her in the eye—in the same way that I would if I was visiting someone's home. Who are the invisible people in your world, and how can you take actions to affirm that they are people created in God's image?

Person	Actions you can take	Actions/behaviors you can reduce

For Further Reflection

Did not he who made me in the womb make them?
    Did not the same one form us both within our mothers? (Job 31:15)

I praise you because I am fearfully and wonderfully made;
    your works are wonderful,
    I know that full well. (Psalm 139:14)

Before I formed you in the womb I knew you,
    before you were born I set you apart. (Jeremiah 1:5)

The LORD does not look at the things people look at. People look at the outward appearance, but the LORD looks at the heart. (1 Samuel 16:7)

You are altogether beautiful, my darling;
    there is no flaw in you. (Song of Songs 4:7)

Shalom and Human Responsibility

We live in an incredibly advanced and sophisticated world. In most cities, even in relatively poor countries, you see great evidence of wealth and success—tall skyscrapers, luxury cars, expensive cell phones and fancy houses. The world has certainly come a long way in the second half of this past century, especially after the two world wars. Yet the realities of life for the vast majority of the world population are quite different. There is a great amount of pain and suffering in individual lives. Abject poverty crushes the hopes and dreams of millions. Lack of educational and vocational opportunities robs millions of young people around the world of their ability to succeed, or even provide the basic necessities for their loved ones. Marriages are breaking down in millions, tearing at the very fabric of societies and communities across the globe. Despite the glitter and glamour of technology and wealth, what stares us in the face is darkness and gloom.

But as we saw in the previous session, that was not God's plan for the world. He called all that he created *good*. And humanity, the jewel of his creation, was right in the center of all that goodness. All of creation existed in perfect harmony and together it existed to bring glory to God.

This session is about God's plan for his creation—shalom—and about the role we have in it.

 Recall

As you've reflected on the last session, how have you felt like an image bearer? What has caused you to not feel like an image bearer?

As an image bearer, what role do you play in God's divine plan for creation?

⊏⊐ Read

Genesis 2:4-25

⁴This is the account of the heavens and the earth when they were created, when the LORD God made the earth and the heavens.

⁵Now no shrub had yet appeared on the earth and no plant had yet sprung up, for the Lord God had not sent rain on the earth and there was no one to work the ground, ⁶but streams came up from the earth and watered the whole surface of the ground. ⁷Then the LORD God formed a man from the dust of the ground and breathed into his nostrils the breath of life, and the man became a living being.

⁸Now the LORD God had planted a garden in the east, in Eden; and there he put the man he had formed. ⁹The LORD God made all kinds of trees grow out of the ground—trees that were pleasing to the eye and good for food. In the middle of the garden were the tree of life and the tree of the knowledge of good and evil.

¹⁰A river watering the garden flowed from Eden; from there it was separated into four headwaters. ¹¹The name of the first is the Pishon; it winds through the entire land of Havilah, where there is gold. ¹²(The gold of that land is good; aromatic resin and onyx are also there.) ¹³The name of the second river is the Gihon; it winds through the entire land of Cush. ¹⁴The name of the third river is the Tigris; it runs along the east side of Ashur. And the fourth river is the Euphrates.

¹⁵The LORD God took the man and put him in the Garden of Eden to work it and take care of it. ¹⁶And the LORD God commanded the man, "You are free to eat from any tree in the garden; ¹⁷but you must not eat from the tree of the knowledge of good and evil, for when you eat of it you will certainly die."

¹⁸The LORD God said, "It is not good for the man to be alone. I will make a helper suitable for him."

¹⁹Now the LORD God had formed out of the ground all the wild animals and all the birds in the sky. He brought them to the man to see what he would name them; and whatever the man called each living creature, that was its name. ²⁰So the man gave names to all the livestock, the birds in the sky and all the wild animals.

But for Adam no suitable helper was found. ²¹So the LORD God caused the man to fall into a deep sleep; and while he was sleeping, he took one of the man's ribs and then closed up the place with flesh. ²²Then the LORD God made a woman from the rib he had taken out of the man, and he brought her to the man.

[23]The man said,

"This is now bone of my bones
    and flesh of my flesh;
she shall be called 'woman,'
    for she was taken out of man."

[24]That is why a man leaves his father and mother and is united to his wife, and they become one flesh.

[25]Adam and his wife were both naked, and they felt no shame.

⚲ Reflect

Now we have a full picture of God's creation—of God's paradise. This holistic picture of the Garden of Eden—of work, of community—is the embodiment of flourishing, of wholeness, of shalom. This Hebrew word, most commonly translated as "peace," is much richer than that. Cornelius Plantinga offers a definition of shalom as being *beyond* peace: "We call it peace, but it means far more than mere peace of mind, or cease-fire among enemies. In the Bible, shalom means universal flourishing, wholeness, and delight."[1] It is life as God intended it. It is life in which there is inner and outer harmony—where humans do what we are created to do while being in right relationship with ourselves, God, others and the environment. God's shalom is the result of goodness and beauty cultivated and lived out. It embraces the full range of relationships that exist to create a whole and abundant life.

■ **Question #1:** How does this passage describe God's relationship to the man? What do we know about the man's relationship to others and to nature? What do we know about God's relationship to nature?

God desires for all people to FLOURISH. Nicholas Wolterstorff describes shalom in this way: "The state of *shalom* is the state of flourishing in all dimensions of one's existence: in one's relation to God, in one's relations to one's fellow human beings, in one's relation to nature, and in one's relation to oneself. Evidently justice has something to do with the fact that God's love for each and every one of God's human creatures takes the form of God desiring the *shalom* of each and every one. Not merely the freedom from violation of one's property, but the flourishing of each and every one."[2]

■ **Question #2:** Since the Garden of Eden was perfect and no sin existed there, why did God tell Adam and Eve that they could not eat of a certain tree?

God is INTENTIONAL. God is intentional in all things. He moves and acts purposefully, setting all things in place, order and motion. God desired that Adam and Eve would live in a garden of beauty, where they would be fully and perfectly cared for, provided for and protected. They would have joyful fellowship with God and with each other. He created a system within which Adam and Eve would live, and in his infinite wisdom he provided them with one boundary: that they could not eat from the tree of the knowledge of good and evil. And he did this to sustain the order and the perfect shalom of the garden. This is the beautiful intentionality of God—that those he created would thrive within his ordered creation. When Adam and Eve stepped out of God's intentional design and decided to sin, shalom was damaged.

Shalom is maintained through setting and keeping BOUNDARIES. Many people are confused as to why God would have to draw boundaries for Adam and Eve in a place where there was no sin. This is an important question to ask! Any love-relationship, even the healthiest and most loving of all, has boundaries.

Jayanthi, an IJM client in India, holds up the first picture she's ever drawn, after being rescued from forced labor in a rock quarry.

In the same way, by placing boundaries in the Garden of Eden, God gave Adam and Eve a chance to continually show their love for him each day. When they chose to be obedient, to stay within the boundary, it showed God that they were committed to loving him, to choosing his ways. It also meant that they could choose each day to trust that God knew what was best for them and that he created things intentionally. The boundaries God set in Eden gave Adam and Eve a way of entering into a deeper and more fruitful love-relationship with him, one where they could be active in the love-relationship with God, and not just passive receivers of his love.

■ **Question #3**: Recall a time when God placed a boundary in your life. What was your response? What purpose did the boundary serve?

The boundaries God sets for us are GOOD. It is interesting to note that boundaries are present in the place that is the most perfect embodiment of shalom, the Garden of Eden. Last session we learned that creation is *good*. This means that the boundaries God sets for us are also good and are meant to lead us to more complete human flourishing. God sets everything good into place.

Shalom brings peace and order to the CENTRAL RELATIONSHIPS of our lives. Shalom should be present in each of these four critical relationships: our relationship with God, our relationship with ourselves, our relationships with others and our relationship with creation.

An IJM social worker hugs Griselda, an IJM client in Guatemala.

This passage illustrates the central relationships that fill our lives and how our peace in those relationships leads to the fullness of shalom. Even in the very first community of the garden, God designed Adam and Eve to be "united" as "one flesh," and they were made to be "helper[s]" to one another. This gives us the clear picture that part of the foundation of human relationships is service and helping one another.

■ **Question #4**: How would you describe a relationship that is characterized by shalom? What do you notice about the people in that relationship or how they interact with those around them?

> "The state of *shalom* is the state of flourishing in all dimensions of one's existence: in one's relation to God, in one's relations to one's fellow human beings, in one's relation to nature, and in one's relation to oneself."
>
> *Nicholas Wolterstorff*

⎯⎯⎯⎯⎯⎯⎯⎯⎯⎯⎯⎯⎯⎯⎯⎯⎯⎯⎯⎯⎯⎯⎯⎯⎯⎯⎯⎯⎯⎯⎯⎯⎯⎯⎯

A little lady named Shukla Bose found that she was very unhappy about the kinds of lives children were leading in the slums of Bangalore, India. Her heart was broken because these children were spending their days begging on the streets, working low-paying jobs at very young ages and going home to broken, often violent families, in communities where 98 percent of fathers were alcoholics. The children lived in such poverty that they didn't have any hope of a better future. Also, people looked down on these slum children. "They cannot learn," they would say. "Slum children cannot be educated; they cannot learn English; they are too dumb." What's more, the government was not helping these children. Ninety percent of government funding for school was spent on teachers' salaries, but at least one in four teachers never showed up to school, not even for one day of the school year.

But Shukla saw the potential in these children. Though their lives were so full of brokenness, she saw a better future for them, a future full of shalom. She decided to start an education program. Even if she only educated one child, she said, it would be a success. Her first school was on a rooftop, right in the heart of one of Bangalore's slums. For the first time, Shukla brought messages of hope and care to these children. She believed that they could do great things, and she was dedicated to not leaving them until they went all the way through school to university. She started teaching them English, a language they would need to know to be global citizens. She set them on a very tough curriculum, which nobody believed they could learn, because she thought that these children deserved the best education possible. The children excelled at this curriculum,

and they mastered English very quickly, some within three months! They even
started teaching their parents. People in the community who said that these
children were too dumb were starting to realize how wrong they had been.

Shukla was also concerned for the children's health. She started a meal program and classes, which provided children with a healthy, balanced diet and
taught them about which foods were good for them to eat. She also started a
sports club for the children so they could get some exercise. The school's team
even won many championships!

But Shukla knew that shalom involves every area of life, including family. She
knew that these children's families were struggling. She arranged for after-
school reading and writing classes so that the parents could also receive education and be involved in their children's lives. She provided training classes for the
alcoholic fathers, where they learned to cook and to have pride in their abilities
as they made good food for their families after such a long period of not providing
for them. Shukla also knew that it was important to give vocational and job training to the older siblings so that they could find better jobs, allowing their younger
siblings the time and resources to go to school. All of the children's parents now
came to teacher meetings to be involved in their children's new community.

With this school, called Parikrma Humanity Foundation, a community of shalom
bloomed in one of the darkest, more hopeless corners of the world. The value of
children is respected, families are brought back together, teachers work not just
for salary but to foster something good in these children and the whole community
has come to work together on this project.[3]

Review

Where do you see shalom in this Indian school?

Respond

Shalom is reflected within four key relationships in our lives: our relationship
to self, God, others and the environment. In which of these relationships is it
hardest to hope for shalom? Why?

Reflect on these four relationships in your own life. How might you move closer to shalom? Select one of these relationships for this exercise. On the chart below, identify the current barriers that keep you from experiencing shalom in this relationship. Then generate some ideas for moving past each barrier. Finally, consider the fruit, or good things, which might result in that relationship once shalom is restored.

Fill in the blank with what you've selected: Relationship to _____

Barriers to shalom	How to move past the barrier	Fruit of shalom restored

For Further Reflection

All peoples on earth will be blessed through you. (Genesis 12:3)

The LORD bless you
    and keep you;
the LORD make his face shine on you
    and be gracious to you;
the LORD turn his face toward you
    and give you peace. (Numbers 6:24-26)

Because I rescued the poor who cried for help,
    and the fatherless who had none to assist them.
The one who was dying blessed me;
    I made the widow's heart sing.
I put on righteousness as my clothing;
    justice was my robe and my turban.
I was eyes to the blind
    and feet to the lame.
I was a father to the needy;
    I took up the case of the stranger. (Job 29:12-16)

The blind receive sight, the lame walk, those who have leprosy are cleansed, the deaf hear, the dead are raised, and the good news is proclaimed to the poor. (Matthew 11:5)

---
③

How Sin Corrupts Shalom

When I (Abraham) was a young boy, about ten years old or so, I remember my parents talking about making some improvements in our kitchen. We were going to have new shelves, new paint, new countertops and—most exciting of all—a beautiful new ceramic kitchen sink. Don't ask me why as a ten-year-old I was excited about an upgraded kitchen. I just was! One day, I remember this kitchen sink sitting on the floor waiting to be installed the next day, and I also remember excitedly jumping about through our home. Then, in almost no time at all, my excited feet landed on the beautiful ceramic sink, shattering it into a thousand pieces. I still remember the horror and shock of that moment, and more than three decades later I can still almost feel the pain.

I wonder if God's pain at his broken creation was anything like that. Perhaps a silly comparison, but of the pain in God's heart we have no doubt. His *good* creation now lay broken and marred by sin and evil.

In the previous session we looked at what shalom involved, and we looked at our own role in God's divine plan for his creation. In this session, we will spend time looking at how sin actually creeps in and corrupts God's beautiful plan. What does sin do? How? Where do we see it today?

↱ Recall

Last session, we discussed the systems and culture that are needed for shalom to flourish. How did God's intentions for shalom emerge in his design of creation?

Recall a time when sin created ruin or destruction in a relationship of your own or of someone close to you. In that situation, what was the sin that generated the destruction?

⌧ Read

Genesis 3:1-13, 21-24; 4:1-12

[1]Now the serpent was more crafty than any of the wild animals the LORD God had made. He said to the woman, "Did God really say, 'You must not eat from any tree in the garden'?"

[2]The woman said to the serpent, "We may eat fruit from the trees in the garden, [3]but God did say, 'You must not eat fruit from the tree that is in the middle of the garden, and you must not touch it, or you will die.'"

[4]"You will not certainly die," the serpent said to the woman. [5]"For God knows that when you eat from it your eyes will be opened, and you will be like God, knowing good and evil."

[6]When the woman saw that the fruit of the tree was good for food and pleasing to the eye, and also desirable for gaining wisdom, she took some and ate it. She also gave some to her husband, who was with her, and he ate it. [7]Then the eyes of both of them were opened, and they realized they were naked; so they sewed fig leaves together and made coverings for themselves.

[8]Then the man and his wife heard the sound of the LORD God as he was walking in the garden in the cool of the day, and they hid from the LORD God among the trees of the garden. [9]But the LORD God called to the man, "Where are you?"

[10]He answered, "I heard you in the garden, and I was afraid because I was naked; so I hid."

[11]And he said, "Who told you that you were naked? Have you eaten from the tree that I commanded you not to eat from?"

[12]The man said, "The woman you put here with me—she gave me some fruit from the tree, and I ate it."

[13]Then the LORD God said to the woman, "What is this you have done?"

The woman said, "The serpent deceived me, and I ate."

[21]The LORD God made garments of skin for Adam and his wife and clothed them. [22]And the LORD God said, "The man has now become like one of us, knowing good and evil. He must not be allowed to reach out his hand and take also from the tree of life and eat, and live forever." [23]So the LORD God banished him from the Garden

of Eden to work the ground from which he had been taken. ²⁴After he drove the man out, he placed on the east side of the Garden of Eden cherubim and a flaming sword flashing back and forth to guard the way to the tree of life.

4 Adam made love to his wife Eve, and she became pregnant and gave birth to Cain. She said, "With the help of the LORD I have brought forth a man." ² Later she gave birth to his brother Abel.

Now Abel kept flocks, and Cain worked the soil. ³In the course of time Cain brought some of the fruits of the soil as an offering to the LORD. ⁴And Abel also brought an offering—fat portions from some of the firstborn of his flock. The LORD looked with favor on Abel and his offering, ⁵but on Cain and his offering he did not look with favor. So Cain was very angry, and his face was downcast.

⁶Then the LORD said to Cain, "Why are you angry? Why is your face downcast? ⁷If you do what is right, will you not be accepted? But if you do not do what is right, sin is crouching at your door; it desires to have you, but you must rule over it."

⁸ Now Cain said to his brother Abel, "Let's go out to the field." While they were in the field, Cain attacked his brother Abel and killed him.

⁹ Then the LORD said to Cain, "Where is your brother Abel?"

"I don't know," he replied. "Am I my brother's keeper?"

¹⁰The LORD said, "What have you done? Listen! Your brother's blood cries out to me from the ground. ¹¹Now you are under a curse and driven from the ground, which opened its mouth to receive your brother's blood from your hand. ¹²When you work the ground, it will no longer yield its crops for you. You will be a restless wanderer on the earth."

⌕ Reflect

- **Question #1**: What do you notice about the serpent's tactics in Genesis 3?

Sin comes about through LIES and DECEPTION. The serpent in this passage snares Adam and Eve with lies and deception. First the serpent introduces doubt: "Did God really say . . . ?" Then Eve misquotes the words of God. God never told Adam and Eve that they could not touch the tree, but Eve tells this to the serpent. Then the serpent makes a bold move and plants the idea in Eve's mind that God might be lying to her and Adam: "You will not certainly die."

Then the serpent brings out his second weapon: he convinces Eve that she and Adam could be *like God*. Adam and Eve have been blessed with the most

beautiful thing one could hope for: relationship with God. Yet the serpent twists this and convinces Adam and Eve that instead of being in relationship with God, they could be *like* God. Adam and Eve forget the intentionality of God, that he has designed their environment and relationships and that they are to serve and to glorify him. Remember that God has purposefully restricted Adam and Eve from having his mind, the knowledge of good and evil. As they fall victim to the belief that they could be like him, conflict and competition develop where there should be trust and cooperation.

The serpent also introduces the lie that God has *not* given Adam and Eve everything they need, but that he has withheld something from them. It introduces the lie that God's creation is not entirely good—that

An IJM social worker in Bolivia comforts a young girl, who has been sexually assaulted.

something is lacking. By causing Adam and Eve to question whether God knows what is best for them and loves them fully, the serpent craftily breaks down their ability to trust God. As a result, the relationship between Adam and Eve and God is damaged, and shalom is broken.

▪ **Question #2**: Why do you think the sin of deception is so destructive to relationships?

Sin breaks down RELATIONSHIPS with God and one another. In Adam and Eve's decision to sin, we see the ways in which God's design for human flourishing is turned upside down. Let's consider God's response to Adam and Eve in the garden. In a broken world, work becomes toil, anxiety-ridden hard labor: "through painful toil you will eat food from it" (Genesis 3:17).

When we read Genesis 4:1-12, we see that the loss of shalom is evident in the lives of Adam and Eve's own children, Cain and Abel. In what appears to be an effort to restore shalom in their relationships with God, both Cain and Abel bring offerings to him. Cain brings some of the fruit he grew and Abel brings an offering of the best of his firstborn sheep. God accepts Abel and his offering but does not "look with favor" on Cain and his offering, though it is unclear exactly why Cain's sacrifice was not accepted. As a result of God's favor toward Abel, Cain is furious and jealous. In a rage, he takes power in his own hands and kills his brother Abel.

Cain violated the God-given dignity and worth of his brother. He took a life which was not his to take. He overstepped the boundary that God created. This is the nature of all sin. It is a rejection of God's design and an embracing of self as supreme.

■ **Question #3:** How is the sin that Adam and Eve committed different from the sin that Cain commits?

Fill in the diagram below. Compare the nature of the sin that Adam and Eve committed with the sin that Cain commits. What are the similarities and differences?

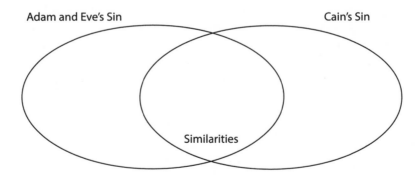

Adam and Eve's Sin   Cain's Sin

Similarities

The sin of INJUSTICE. Cain commits a particular type of sin: injustice. The sin of injustice is when one person uses his or her power to take the life or liberties away from another. God's reaction to the murder of Abel demonstrates his anger over the violation and destruction of another human life. God loves justice and proclaims that it belongs to him and that he desires it for all. Justice is a part of God's character, a vital part of who God is. He created justice that is good and that seeks to sustain shalom. Injustice, on the other hand, furthers destruction and broken relationships.

A prison in Kenya where hundreds are illegally detained and waiting for justice.

We must realize the difference of Cain's sin from Adam and Eve's sin. Cain's sin is a direct form of injustice toward others: the rejection of the sanctity of life. The sin of injustice today is committed by those who, like Cain, violate the dignity of others, removing from them the opportunity to thrive and flourish.

Injustice is seen very clearly in the different types of evil that International Justice Mission combats. In cases of slavery, the joy and glory of work is turned into a power struggle of hard labor for the personal gain of a single individual. In cases of forced prostitution, what God intended to be an act of the deepest and most trusting of human relationships also becomes a power struggle—the strong taking from the weak rather than each person uplifting one another. In cases of property grabbing, the relationship between humans and the land is corrupted. Rather than the land being a source of nourishment for a widow and her children, it is turned into a source of profit for another family, and the relationship between humans and the land is broken. In all of these examples, we see how relationships intended for mutual support are turned into power struggles of the strong against the weak.

> Injustice is when one person uses his or her power to take the life or liberties away from another.

Nearly thirty-six million people are trapped in slavery today.[1] As we encounter such a staggering number, we must also remember that the statistic represents millions of individual lives. People who are victims of human trafficking worldwide see very real examples of how lies and deception destroy shalom.

Theerthagiri, his wife Lakshmi and their three children lived a difficult, but peaceful life in South India. Theerthagiri worked in construction, and while the family didn't have many belongings, they were able to make ends meet. However, like many Indian families, Theerthagiri took a small loan when his family needed a small amount of extra funds—in this case, he and Lakshmi were planning an important cultural celebration for one of their daughters.

Theerthagiri later struggled to pay off this small debt—about $200 US dollars—and faced pressure from the money lender to repay him or have a heavier interest imposed. Theerthagiri became increasingly desperate and anxious. During that time, he met the owner of a brick kiln who offered a solution that would enable Theerthagiri to provide for his family and repay the loan; he would clear the debt if Theerthagiri would come and work at his brick kiln.

Theerthagiri, his wife Lakshmi and their teenage daughter Vaneshawari embraced this opportunity, moving to the kiln. But Theerthagiri quickly came to a terrible realization: the seemingly generous offer the facility owner made to him was simply a trick intended to trap him in forced labor. He, his wife and his daughter became slaves.

The owner locked them in a room at night, not allowing them to use the restroom until morning; they were not allowed to leave the facility unless accompanied by one of the owner's men. Even when a close relative passed away, Theerthagiri and Lakshmi were forced to leave Vaneshawari behind as a surety for their return in order to attend the funeral back at their native village. The owner also beat and threatened to burn the laborers alive with kerosene. Desperate to get his family out of the abusive kiln, a distressed Theerthagiri told the owner he would pay him back by accepting a loan from someone else. But the owner said he was uninterested in his money—he only wanted their labor. He went on to say that he was not planning to ever let them go, even if they repaid him in full. The loan the owner made was only a small expense for ensuring their free labor permanently. Theerthagiri feared he'd die before being rescued.

This is the sad reality of how lies and deceit break the shalom of healthy human flourishing every day. An intricate web of lies and manipulation led Theerthagiri and his family into a den of evil.

But, as we have seen, there is grace! Some IJM investigators heard about the case. After a lengthy undercover investigation, they were able to free Theerthagiri and his family. They now have honest jobs and their children can go to school. God's grace is profound![2]

💡 Review

Why is the sin of injustice so destructive to shalom?

🙶 Respond

How is your understanding and awareness of injustice beginning to change?

For Further Reflection

Again I looked and saw all the oppression that was taking place under the sun:

I saw the tears of the oppressed—
    and they have no comforter;
power was on the side of their oppressors—
    and they have no comforter. (Ecclesiastes 4:1)

The LORD detests lying lips,
    but he delights in people who are trustworthy. (Proverbs 12:22)

You have been a refuge for the poor,
    a refuge for the needy in their distress,
a shelter from the storm
    and a shade from the heat. (Isaiah 25:4)

On this mountain he will destroy
    the shroud that enfolds all peoples,
the sheet that covers all nations;
    he will swallow up death forever.
The Sovereign LORD will wipe away the tears
    from all faces;
he will remove his people's disgrace
    from all the earth.
        The LORD has spoken. (Isaiah 25:7-8)

4

Personal and Systemic Injustice

Walking through the streets of any city in the world today, one could easily identify a great deal of injustice. IJM's lawyers and social workers work with some of the most grievous cases of injustice in several countries in the developing world. The examples and stories are too many to count. Sadly, such stories of abuse are not limited only to poor countries in the developing world. The effects of sin and evil are everywhere, even in the richest countries in the world.

Most of us are revolted and deeply saddened by such stories of abuse and injustice. There are other injustices, however, that are not as easily visible and therefore often go unnoticed. These injustices are embedded in corrupt systems and processes. When you think about it, these are equally awful. Whether it is a corrupt court system where a common citizen would be unlikely to find justice, a police force that protects only those who could afford to pay a bribe, a local official who would turn a blind eye to the violent abuse of a helpless widow or a village where—despite government funding—the schools discriminate against children from a certain group leaving them susceptible to a lifetime of illiteracy, poverty and abuse. All of these are as despicable as the stories of individual abuse, and yet these are often condoned, or at least tolerated.

This session will allow us the opportunity to look at systematic injustice and will cause us to think about sources of evil and abuse in our own communities. It is our responsibility as Christ-followers to identify and stand against injustice, wherever we find it.

⤤ Recall

Last session, we discussed the sin that Cain committed against Abel and how deeply unjust that was. Based on what you learned, write a definition of injustice in your own words.

Injustice is:

Today, we'll focus on another story of injustice, but we'll look at how this injustice was allowed because of oppressive cultural norms in society and a system that could not protect Tamar.

⊏⊐ Read

Genesis 38:6-26

⁶Judah got a wife for Er, his firstborn, and her name was Tamar. ⁷But Er, Judah's firstborn, was wicked in the LORD's sight; so the LORD put him to death.

⁸Then Judah said to Onan, "Sleep with your brother's wife and fulfill your duty to her as a brother-in-law to raise up offspring for your brother." ⁹But Onan knew that the child would not be his; so whenever he slept with his brother's wife, he spilled his semen on the ground to keep from providing offspring for his brother. ¹⁰What he did was wicked in the LORD's sight; so the LORD put him to death also.

¹¹Judah then said to his daughter-in-law Tamar, "Live as a widow in your father's household until my son Shelah grows up." For he thought, "He may die too, just like his brothers." So Tamar went to live in her father's household.

¹²After a long time Judah's wife, the daughter of Shua, died. When Judah had recovered from his grief, he went up to Timnah, to the men who were shearing his sheep, and his friend Hirah the Adullamite went with him.

¹³When Tamar was told, "Your father-in-law is on his way to Timnah to shear his sheep," ¹⁴she took off her widow's clothes, covered herself with a veil to disguise herself, and then sat down at the entrance to Enaim, which is on the road to Timnah. For she saw that, though Shelah had now grown up, she had not been given to him as his wife.

¹⁵When Judah saw her, he thought she was a prostitute, for she had covered her face. ¹⁶Not realizing that she was his daughter-in-law, he went over to her by the roadside and said, "Come now, let me sleep with you."

"And what will you give me to sleep with you?" she asked.

¹⁷"I'll send you a young goat from my flock," he said.

"Will you give me something as a pledge until you send it?" she asked.

¹⁸He said, "What pledge should I give you?"

"Your seal and its cord, and the staff in your hand," she answered. So he gave them to her and slept with her, and she became pregnant by him. ¹⁹After she left, she took off her veil and put on her widow's clothes again.

²⁰Meanwhile Judah sent the young goat by his friend the Adullamite in order to get his pledge back from the woman, but he did not find her. ²¹He asked the men

who lived there, "Where is the shrine prostitute who was beside the road at Enaim?"

"There hasn't been any shrine prostitute here," they said.

²²So he went back to Judah and said, "I didn't find her. Besides, the men who lived there said, 'There hasn't been any shrine prostitute here.'"

²³Then Judah said, "Let her keep what she has, or we will become a laughing-stock. After all, I did send her this young goat, but you didn't find her."

²⁴About three months later Judah was told, "Your daughter-in-law Tamar is guilty of prostitution, and as a result she is now pregnant."

Judah said, "Bring her out and have her burned to death!"

²⁵As she was being brought out, she sent a message to her father-in-law. "I am pregnant by the man who owns these," she said. And she added, "See if you recognize whose seal and cord and staff these are."

²⁶Judah recognized them and said, "She is more righteous than I, since I wouldn't give her to my son Shelah." And he did not sleep with her again.

Reflect

- **Question #1:** What surprises you about this story?

What types of injustice do you see in this passage?

What evidence do you see of Tamar's vulnerability to neglect and oppression in this passage? For each verse below, record what you find:

Genesis 38:11:

Genesis 38:14:

Genesis 38:15-16:

Genesis 38:24:

Systems within SOCIETY and CULTURE can contribute to injustice. In order to understand this story, we need to know some background. In Hebrew tradition, family was extremely important, so to be widowed and left alone was to have absolutely no place in society. Tamar was far away from her family, she could not get a job and since she had been married before, it was extremely unlikely that any gentleman in the community would choose her for a bride. To protect women like Tamar, it was the duty of the brother of a deceased man to marry his widowed sister-in-law so she could remain under the protection of the family. Remember that Tamar is probably about fifteen years old when this story starts, yet at such a young age her life is basically over.

In this passage, we see that Tamar is the victim of cultural injustice, not just one person's sin against her. Because she is a widow, she is vulnerable in society. Her status in society denies her some of the opportunities and provision that she needs to flourish. We must be careful not to interpret this story as justifying any type of sin, but instead we must read it as an illustration of how important justice is to God and how dangerous it can be when injustice is allowed to flourish unchecked.

▪ **Question #2:** What societal obstacles exist for Tamar?

What choices does Judah make that relate to the mistreatment of Tamar?

What enables Judah to make these choices? What does he possess that Tamar does not?

Personal injustice happens because of the misuse of POWER and PRIVILEGE. Judah perpetuates injustice against Tamar. We see him sending Tamar off to "wait" for his youngest son to grow up without actually intending to follow through on his promise. In fact, Judah deceives Tamar by promising her something he has no intention of fulfilling. Similarly to Cain, Judah is focused on himself.

Judah's power and privilege is derived from his wealth and status in the community. As a poor widow, Tamar is powerless. Judah's position means he can help her, yet he decides to deal with her life in a careless way. He abandons her, exploits her and violates her because his desire to maintain power is greater than his desire to respect and honor human life.

Individuals can commit injustice, but systems can also PERPETUATE injustice or selectively disadvantage some members. In his teaching on this passage, Pastor Tim Keller explains that in order for Tamar to have succeeded with her plan, she must have known that Judah was a man who would sleep with a prostitute wherever he found one. In other words, Judah did not hesitate to commit adultery on a regular basis.[1] However, when Judah finds out that Tamar committed adultery, he orders her to be burned to death, a much more cruel and painful punishment than was stipulated for such an act. He refuses to be accountable for his behavior, but condemns Tamar for the same sin. She does not have an advocate or any opportunity to lodge a complaint or accusation against Judah. There is no system within which Tamar can seek justice for herself. There is no place for her to plead her case. As a woman, Tamar is doubly disadvantaged: she is sentenced to a much more severe penalty for her crime because of her gender, and she does

Undercover photo by an IJM investigator of young girls being held in a brothel in Southeast Asia.

not have power in that society to defend herself against the accusations of a man.

The economic system during Tamar's time did not allow good options of survival for women who were not married or not a part of a family. Later on, God's law established a system to counteract that injustice—the command for younger sons to marry their brother's wife (and thus re-establish her role under the protection of the family). This is an example of God instituting a system to counteract an unjust economic system.

This is a pattern we see in our societies today and it is deeply unfair. Many perpetrators of injustice are more than happy to enslave or prostitute others but they would be horrified to be put in that position themselves. And punishment is often skewed differently to different types of people for the same crime. Because of the chronic lack of accountability for perpetrators in many countries and ineffective justice systems, those who oppress the vulnerable routinely go unpunished. The lack of functioning legal systems leaves millions of people without protection or any type of advocacy. When perpetrators go unrestrained, injustice is allowed to flourish and those with power and privilege can act without any consequences for their treatment of the oppressed.

■ **Question #3:** What does Judah's declaration in verse 26 teach us about justice?

The story of Tamar is full of sin. No one in this passage is blameless, but in the end Tamar becomes the heroine as she bravely endures both personal and systemic injustice. This is not to say that Tamar's sin is overlooked. Notice, Judah does not deem her blameless at the end, but he says, she is *more* righteous than I, and he recognizes his sin of injustice.

God is not justifying prostitution through this passage of Scripture, but he is asking us to recognize the greater danger and the greater sadness of injustice and inequality in society, a society where widows are neglected and people with power conform to the law, only as it is convenient.

■ **Question #4:** Who are the vulnerable people in your society today?

What obstacles exist for these people? Are there any systems where they are penalized? How are they generally viewed by society?

What is in place to counteract systemic inequality?

This passage shows us our responsibility to recognize injustice in the SYSTEMS in society. When Judah fails to provide a husband for Tamar, he is condemning her to a life without hope or future. He had the means to help her, but he chose not to. To live in a society where the built-in systems leave people poor, weak and looked down on and to not do anything about it is to engage in injustice, especially when we have the means—no matter how little—to speak out against the structures which create inequalities in our societies. These unequal structures may be bad public education systems which deny the same opportunities to the poor. They may be social pressures which deem one sector or caste of society as less valuable or less worthy of care than another. They may be unjust labor laws which force the poor to work for extremely low wages. Whatever the injustice looks like, God holds us responsible for using our gifts and resources to fight against it. Proverbs 3:27 commands us, "Do not withhold good from those to whom it is due, when it is in your power to act."

During World War II, Denmark was occupied by the German Nazis. The Danes were determined to save their Jews from the fate that had met so many other European Jews under Nazi occupation, so in households, streets and villages an operation began to hide Danish Jews and then smuggle them out to Sweden in the north, which remained neutral during the war.

However, Sweden had not been so willing to provide asylum to Jews. They had already turned away the Norwegian Jews who had attempted to find asylum there. But the Danish people knew this was the only hope for their Jews. If they did not get them out of Denmark, they would soon be discovered by the occupying Nazi forces.

But hope came in the form of a Danish physicist, Niels Bohr, who later flew to the United States to work on a project with the world's most renowned scientists. Germany invaded Denmark in 1940. In 1943, Bohr fled to Sweden to escape deportation. When his plane touched down in Sweden, government representatives tried to get him to board a plane to the United States where he should have been going, but Bohr refused. Instead, he promised that he would not leave Swedish soil until the King had announced publicly, through every possible medium of the press, that Sweden would offer asylum. Indeed, four days later it was broadcast on the airwaves that Sweden would accept Denmark's Jews. Soon after, Bohr flew to America, and the Danes started a historic process of smuggling their Jews on boats across the water that separates Denmark and Sweden.[2]

Even though two out of every three Jews died in the Holocaust, 99 percent of Denmark's Jews escaped the Nazis and survived. Even though Bohr was not a politician, military commander or a member of the royal family, he recognized injustice and the need for a strong, free country to defend the oppressed, and he stuck his neck out to secure the safety of Denmark's Jews.

Review

How does the story of Niels Bohr illustrate the ability of people to change a system?

Respond

We've now discussed the way that injustice can be committed through a system in society. What has challenged you or what have you learned?

What systems are you a part of? Is there anything that you can do in the place where you are to extend justice? (Example: A student, alumni or parent might advocate for changes in the educational system for those who are most vulnerable.)

For Further Reflection

Do not withhold good from those to whom it is due,
    when it is in your power to act.
Do not say to your neighbor,
    "Come back tomorrow and I'll give it to you"—
    when you already have it with you.
Do not plot harm against your neighbor,
    who lives trustfully near you.
Do not accuse anyone for no reason—
    when they have done you no harm. (Proverbs 3:27-30)

Woe to those who make unjust laws,
    to those who issue oppressive decrees,
to deprive the poor of their rights
    and withhold justice from the oppressed of my people. (Isaiah 10:1-2)

"Teacher, which is the greatest commandment in the Law?"

Jesus replied: "'Love the Lord your God with all your heart and with all your soul and with all your mind.' This is the first and greatest commandment. And the second is like it: 'Love your neighbor as yourself.' All the Law and the Prophets hang on these two commandments." (Matthew 22:36-40)

AFRICA—KAMPALA, UGANDA

RAMONA'S STORY

Several years ago, Ramona* was bullied by her relatives to leave her home and give up her children. When they took her farmland—her family's only source of food and income—she struggled to feed her children or keep them in school. Fortunately, IJM heard Ramona's story in 2011 and stood up for her rights. IJM attorneys helped stop the threats against her and secured her land with official boundary markers in December 2012. It seemed she was safe at last.

However, as Ramona began to return to normal life, setting up a small shop to sell vegetables she grew, an-

Ramona

other relative tried to force her from the land. He destroyed the boundary markers IJM had planted and made astonishing threats of violence to the young mother: he promised to kill her children with a machete, one by one, if she refused to leave. Ramona was rightfully terrified. Just when she thought their troubles with their home were over, they were once again afraid to stay. She says, "Every time my children saw [that relative], they were so scared—and I felt powerless."

IJM took on Ramona's case again. They started by hiring private security to protect Ramona and her children. Then IJM attorneys and investigators began working with police to plan an arrest. But when the relative heard about this, he tried to avoid being punished. He apologized to Ramona on his knees, saying he would replant the markers and leave her alone if she would drop the case. But Ramona could not forget the terrified looks on her children's faces and the fear that this man had brought into their lives. She stood firm.

In an operation carefully planned by IJM and local police, this man was arrested and brought to jail. The very next day he was charged with threatening violence and removing a widow's boundary markers. These charges carry a sentence of up to seven years in prison. His trial is ongoing, but the good news is this man can no longer threaten Ramona and her children, who are now able to live in peace and without fear. Ramona knows his arrest has sent a strong reminder to her in-laws and neighbors that it is wrong to abuse women like her.

*A pseudonym has been used for the protection of this IJM client.

5

The Justice of God

As I (Abraham) began working with churches across the globe to encourage and facilitate their engagement with the work of justice in their communities, one of the biggest surprises for me was the almost passive response of pastors and church leaders to real, actual instances of abuse and oppression. Often when I would hear stories of a little child being sexually abused or a poor, old widow being violently robbed of her meager possessions and left to fend for herself, I would inquire both about the victim and the perpetrator. While all felt the pain of the victim, it was the attitude toward the perpetrator that was mind-boggling to me. They seemed almost indifferent to the fact that the perpetrators had not suffered any consequences for their crime. I would often be told that life for the alleged abuser was almost the same as it was before the abuse because they had been forgiven.

As Christians, we are all acutely aware of the saving grace and forgiveness we have experienced in our own lives, but we often tend to overlook the cost, the punishment. While our own grace and forgiveness from God was unmerited, we cannot overlook the price that was paid on that cross on the hills of Golgotha. Punishment for the wrongs committed is not an unbiblical concept, in fact it is quite the contrary.

This session invites us into a deeper understanding of the heart of God toward evil and injustice: he hates evil and loves justice, he requires us to be the channels of that justice, and punishment for the abuse and oppression of the poor and the weak is a part of God's plan.

Recall

Last session we discussed injustice that happens within our society. How do you think God might bring about justice to a society where people are abused or exploited?

⌨ Read

Exodus 2:23–3:15; 12:29-36; 14:19-31

[23]During that long period, the king of Egypt died. The Israelites groaned in their slavery and cried out, and their cry for help because of their slavery went up to God. [24]God heard their groaning and he remembered his covenant with Abraham, with Isaac and with Jacob. [25]So God looked on the Israelites and was concerned about them.

3 Now Moses was tending the flock of Jethro his father-in-law, the priest of Midian, and he led the flock to the far side of the wilderness and came to Horeb, the mountain of God. [2]There the angel of the LORD appeared to him in flames of fire from within a bush. Moses saw that though the bush was on fire it did not burn up. [3]So Moses thought, "I will go over and see this strange sight—why the bush does not burn up."

[4]When the LORD saw that he had gone over to look, God called to him from within the bush, "Moses! Moses!"

And Moses said, "Here I am."

[5]"Do not come any closer," God said. "Take off your sandals, for the place where you are standing is holy ground." [6]Then he said, "I am the God of your father, the God of Abraham, the God of Isaac and the God of Jacob." At this, Moses hid his face, because he was afraid to look at God.

[7]The LORD said, "I have indeed seen the misery of my people in Egypt. I have heard them crying out because of their slave drivers, and I am concerned about their suffering. [8]So I have come down to rescue them from the hand of the Egyptians and to bring them up out of that land into a good and spacious land, a land flowing with milk and honey—the home of the Canaanites, Hittites, Amorites, Perizzites, Hivites and Jebusites. [9]And now the cry of the Israelites has reached me, and I have seen the way the Egyptians are oppressing them. [10]So now, go. I am sending you to Pharaoh to bring my people the Israelites out of Egypt."

[11]But Moses said to God, "Who am I that I should go to Pharaoh and bring the Israelites out of Egypt?"

[12]And God said, "I will be with you. And this will be the sign to you that it is I who have sent you: When you have brought the people out of Egypt, you will worship God on this mountain."

[13]Moses said to God, "Suppose I go to the Israelites and say to them, 'The God of your fathers has sent me to you,' and they ask me, 'What is his name?' Then what shall I tell them?"

[14]God said to Moses, "I AM WHO I AM. This is what you are to say to the Israelites: 'I AM has sent me to you.'"

[15]God also said to Moses, "Say to the Israelites, 'The LORD, the God of your fathers—the God of Abraham, the God of Isaac and the God of Jacob—has sent me to you.'

"This is my name forever,
the name you shall call me
from generation to generation.

12 At midnight the LORD struck down all the firstborn in Egypt, from the firstborn of Pharaoh, who sat on the throne, to the firstborn of the prisoner, who was in the dungeon, and the firstborn of all the livestock as well. ³⁰Pharaoh and all his officials and all the Egyptians got up during the night, and there was loud wailing in Egypt, for there was not a house without someone dead.

³¹During the night Pharaoh summoned Moses and Aaron and said, "Up! Leave my people, you and the Israelites! Go, worship the LORD as you have requested. ³²Take your flocks and herds, as you have said, and go. And also bless me."

³³The Egyptians urged the people to hurry and leave the country. "For otherwise," they said, "we will all die!" ³⁴So the people took their dough before the yeast was added, and carried it on their shoulders in kneading troughs wrapped in clothing. ³⁵The Israelites did as Moses instructed and asked the Egyptians for articles of silver and gold and for clothing. ³⁶The LORD had made the Egyptians favorably disposed toward the people, and they gave them what they asked for; so they plundered the Egyptians.

14 Then the angel of God, who had been traveling in front of Israel's army, withdrew and went behind them. The pillar of cloud also moved from in front and stood behind them, ²⁰coming between the armies of Egypt and Israel. Throughout the night the cloud brought darkness to the one side and light to the other side; so neither went near the other all night long.

²¹Then Moses stretched out his hand over the sea, and all that night the LORD drove the sea back with a strong east wind and turned it into dry land. The waters were divided, ²²and the Israelites went through the sea on dry ground, with a wall of water on their right and on their left.

²³The Egyptians pursued them, and all Pharaoh's horses and chariots and horsemen followed them into the sea. ²⁴During the last watch of the night the LORD looked down from the pillar of fire and cloud at the Egyptian army and threw it into confusion. ²⁵He jammed the wheels of their chariots so that they had difficulty driving. And the Egyptians said, "Let's get away from the Israelites! The LORD is fighting for them against Egypt."

²⁶Then the LORD said to Moses, "Stretch out your hand over the sea so that the waters may flow back over the Egyptians and their chariots and horsemen." ²⁷Moses stretched out his hand over the sea, and at daybreak the sea went back to its place. The Egyptians were fleeing toward it, and the LORD swept them into the sea. ²⁸The water flowed back and covered the chariots and horsemen—the entire army of Pharaoh that had followed the Israelites into the sea. Not one of them survived.

²⁹But the Israelites went through the sea on dry ground, with a wall of water on

their right and on their left. ³⁰That day the Lord saved Israel from the hands of the Egyptians, and Israel saw the Egyptians lying dead on the shore. ³¹And when the Israelites saw the mighty hand of the Lord displayed against the Egyptians, the people feared the Lord and put their trust in him and in Moses his servant.

🔍 Reflect

This is one of the most epic stories in the Bible illustrating God's heart for justice. The deliverance of the Israelites has ripple effects throughout Scripture, all the way to the birth of Jesus. In many ways, this story illustrates for us God's remarkable rescue and redemption, a pattern that is repeated throughout history all the way to the central story of Christ's sacrifice to save humanity.

- **Question #1:** What do we learn about the character of God from these passages? Complete the chart below.

Verses	God's words or actions	What we learn about God's heart for justice
Exodus 2:24-25		
Exodus 3:7-10		
Exodus 3:19-20		
Exodus 14:24-25		

Understanding the depth of God's HEART for justice. This story of the Israelites' rescue from Egypt reveals so many attributes of God. Most importantly, we see a God who cares about his people and hates to see them suffer. He explicitly says to Moses, "I have indeed seen the misery of my people in Egypt. I have heard them crying out because of their slave drivers, and I am concerned about their suffering. So I have come down to rescue them from the hand of the Egyptians and to bring them up out of that land into a good and spacious land, a land flowing with milk and honey" (Exodus 3:7-8). We see how God cares for his people every step of the way, even parting the sea for them when they are trapped.

We learn that God uses his immense power for the work of justice. This story is full of awesome and miraculous wonders! We see that God works justice in big ways, enabling the refugee migration of an entire people group. But he also works justice in small ways. We see Egyptian neighbors giving their household goods to the Israelites as they leave, a small sign of justice from the Egyptians who had enslaved the Israelites without pay for so long. This passage should give us hope that God is not deaf to our cries and the pleas of the oppressed. God sees, God acts and God redeems.

■ **Question #2**: How do you feel reading the passage and realizing that so many Egyptians had to die? What is the role of punishment in delivering justice?

God's justice involves PUNISHMENT. It is very hard to reconcile a just, loving God with all the punishment we see going on in this story. Around the world today, so much injustice happens in places where those who enslave, rape or abuse others are never held accountable before the law. As we discussed in the previous session, ineffective justice systems actually *enable* injustice rather than prevent it. Perpetrators of these crimes are rarely punished or stopped by police. By holding these perpetrators accountable, the message they receive is clear: you cannot commit a crime without consequences.

■ **Question #3**: What qualifies God to enact punishment on Egypt? Read the following verses and record your thoughts.

Exodus 3:4-7

Exodus 3:14-15

■ **Question #4:** What might have happened to the Israelites if the Lord had not punished Egypt?

Punishment can PREVENT further injustice. A lack of punishment incites more people to injustice because there are no negative consequences, but high reward for the perpetrator. However, IJM has seen that even a few convictions of traffickers, slave owners or abusers can have a massive impact on whether or not other people engage in these crimes. When people think there is even the smallest chance that they might get caught and imprisoned for their crimes, they are much less likely to engage in such behavior in the first place. For the same reason, God had to punish the Egyptians for their crimes so that the peoples around them would be warned of the consequences of enslaving other people. When we first consider this episode, the mass deaths seem cruel, but they actually show another side of God's heart for justice: he desires to stop injustice before it even happens.

■ **Question #5:** What do you think was God's purpose in using Moses to rescue the Israelites?

God works justice THROUGH HIS PEOPLE. This is really hard to understand. Honestly, this one is baffling. Why would God choose to work through his people to accomplish things that he could do much more easily without having to deal with our flaws and brokenness? We learn elsewhere in Exodus that Moses murdered a man before fleeing Egypt. He also has problems with his speech. Why would God use such a flawed person? We cannot pretend to know the full answer to this, but we do know that God promises his people, "I will be with you." God may use us, broken people, to accomplish the work of justice, but we do it in his power and with him by our side.

God graciously includes us in the work of justice so that we too can become people "after God's own heart." To engage in this work is to learn more about

God and to become more like him, bit by bit. We may never fully understand why an all-powerful God would choose to work through weak and flawed people, yet we know that when God calls us into this work—though it is hard—we and our communities will be blessed.

It is hard to believe, but thousands of years after God rescued the Israelites from Egypt there are still people held in slavery, making bricks exactly the same way that the Israelites made them with mud and straw.

Shankar was one of the millions held in modern-day slavery. His work day began before dawn at two or three o'clock in the morning. Every day, Shankar was forced to carry raw, unbaked bricks on his head to the kiln where they would be baked. This is an unimaginably heavy weight, yet Shankar and his wife would carry out this task day after day. If they tired or slowed down, they were beaten by the supervisor who was verbally and physically abusive. The lives of Shankar and his wife were stolen from them. But God heard their cries.

One day, IJM investigators heard about Shankar's story. They were able to contact four of the laborers inside the brick kiln and gather enough evidence to conduct a rescue mission. On July 1, 2009, IJM staff and local officials drove to the brick kiln. They told the laborers to collect their belongings. They would be leaving this place for good! Sixty-six people, including Shankar and his wife and a baby that had been born that very morning, were rescued.

The same day, the Indian government issued release certificates for the laborers, authorizing their freedom and canceling their debts. Shankar and his wife along with the sixty-four other people could start their life anew. Shalom had been restored! Once again, God used his people to bring about justice for the oppressed.[1]

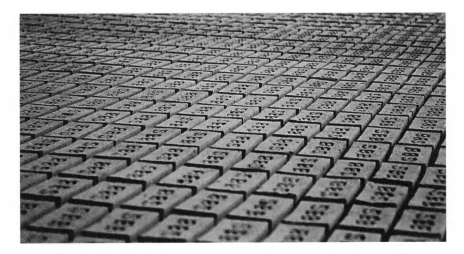

💡 Review

In light of what you've learned in today's session, how would you describe God's response to injustice?

❝❝ Respond

Read Exodus 3:11. What does this verse tell you about how Moses was feeling in response to God's call? One a scale of 1-5, how prepared are you to respond to God's invitation that we seek justice on behalf of others?

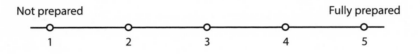

Not prepared   Fully prepared

1   2   3   4   5

How might you further prepare yourself to act?

How does this passage challenge you in your understanding of God's character? How might this cause you to think or behave differently?

For Further Reflection

The LORD himself goes before you and will be with you; he will never leave you nor forsake you. Do not be afraid; do not be discouraged. (Deuteronomy 31:8)

He rescued me from my powerful enemy,
    from my foes, who were too strong for me. (2 Samuel 22:18)

An IJM staff member leads former slaves out of forced labor in a woodcutting facility in India.

He is the Maker of heaven and earth,
    the sea, and everything in them—
    he remains faithful forever.
He upholds the cause of the oppressed
    and gives food to the hungry.
The LORD sets prisoners free,
    the LORD gives sight to the blind,
the LORD lifts up those who are bowed down,
    the LORD loves the righteous.
The LORD watches over the foreigner
    and sustains the fatherless and the widow,
        but he frustrates the ways of the wicked. (Psalm 146:6-9)

Jesus Messiah—New Creation

Often, when we read of or encounter instances of injustice in the world, our thoughts almost naturally drift toward the future hope of the new creation. That hope of God's shalom in the distant future is a precious gift that assures and comforts us that all the pains and agonies of today will someday be wiped away. It is this hope that often sustains us when we are in the depths of despair for a world that seems to be sinking deeper into brokenness with each passing year.

But there are two other truths that make it even better for us. First, God always keeps his promises. His Word promises time and again that he will bring deliverance and relief to those that suffer. There is a bright dawn right behind the night! Second, God is not only concerned about bringing relief and salvation in the distant future, but indeed he has promised tangible justice in the present—freedom for prisoners, sight for the blind and liberty for the oppressed (Luke 4:18-19).

IJM's work in Kenya is proof of this. Our lawyers and social workers labor day and night to bring rescue and restoration to hundreds that have been falsely imprisoned and oppressed. He has called us to this divine cause in Nairobi, Kenya, because that is his will and plan for all creation. Jesus claims that his mission in this world reflects the Father's heart for the poor and the oppressed as well as his plans to bring shalom into this broken world.

⤷ Recall

Last session we discussed God's heart for justice and the ways that he uses people to bring about justice in the world. How central do you think the work of justice was to Christ's purpose on earth?

⊑⊐ Read

Isaiah 61:1-3

[1]The Spirit of the Sovereign Lord is on me,
     because the Lord has anointed me
     to proclaim good news to the poor.
He has sent me to bind up the brokenhearted,
     to proclaim freedom for the captives
     and release from darkness for the prisoners,
[2]to proclaim the year of the Lord's favor
     and the day of vengeance of our God,
to comfort all who mourn,
     [3]and provide for those who grieve in Zion—
to bestow on them a crown of beauty
     instead of ashes,
the oil of joy
     instead of mourning,
and a garment of praise
     instead of a spirit of despair.

Luke 4:1-21

[1]Jesus, full of the Holy Spirit, left the Jordan and was led by the Spirit into the wilderness, [2]where for forty days he was tempted by the devil. He ate nothing during those days, and at the end of them he was hungry.

[3]The devil said to him, "If you are the Son of God, tell this stone to become bread."

[4]Jesus answered, "It is written: 'Man shall not live on bread alone.'"

[5]The devil led him up to a high place and showed him in an instant all the kingdoms of the world. [6]And he said to him, "I will give you all their authority and splendor; it has been given to me, and I can give it to anyone I want to. [7]If you worship me, it will all be yours."

[8]Jesus answered, "It is written: 'Worship the Lord your God and serve him only.'"

[9]The devil led him to Jerusalem and had him stand on the highest point of the temple. "If you are the Son of God," he said, "throw yourself down from here. [10]For it is written:

   "'He will command his angels concerning you
        to guard you carefully;
   [11]they will lift you up in their hands,
        so that you will not strike your foot against a stone.'"

[12]Jesus answered, "It is said: 'Do not put the Lord your God to the test.'"

[13]When the devil had finished all this tempting, he left him until an opportune time.

[14]Jesus returned to Galilee in the power of the Spirit, and news about him spread

through the whole countryside. [15]He was teaching in their synagogues, and everyone praised him.

[16]He went to Nazareth, where he had been brought up, and on the Sabbath day he went into the synagogue, as was his custom. He stood up to read, [17]and the scroll of the prophet Isaiah was handed to him. Unrolling it, he found the place where it is written:

> [18]"The Spirit of the Lord is on me,
>   because he has anointed me
>   to proclaim good news to the poor.
> He has sent me to proclaim freedom for the prisoners
>   and recovery of sight for the blind,
>   to set the oppressed free,
>   [19]to proclaim the year of the Lord's favor."

[20]Then he rolled up the scroll, gave it back to the attendant and sat down. The eyes of everyone in the synagogue were fastened on him. [21]He began by saying to them, "Today this scripture is fulfilled in your hearing."

Reflect

The tide is turning in the story of justice! This week we see the beginning of God's ultimate rescue mission to restore shalom by sending his son Jesus Christ to live the kind of life that we should have lived. Jesus makes it very clear that he has come to bring redemption and justice in tangible ways, right here on earth, right now. As imitators of Christ, we should take inspiration and hope from Christ's example.

▪ **Question #1**: Look back at session 3 and re-read Genesis 3:1-7. What similarities do you see between the passage in Luke and the temptation in the Garden of Eden? What differences do you see?

Jesus comes to restore SHALOM and the perfection of Eden. This passage is the New Testament retelling of the tragic story in Genesis 3, when Adam and Eve were tempted by the serpent into rejecting God. We find Jesus in a desert as he is being tempted by the very same devil who tricked Adam and Eve, using the very same tricks on Jesus that he pulled on them. He is trying to twist the truth and get Jesus to doubt God's love for him. He tries to make Jesus question who he is: "If you are the Son of God . . ." He also tries to disable Jesus' trust in God by getting him to rely on earthly things instead: "Tell this stone to become bread," says the devil, trying to undermine Jesus' faith that God will sustain him.

■ **Question #2**: In both passages, what is the lure that Satan uses to tempt Adam and Eve and then Jesus?

Passage	Lure Satan uses to tempt
Genesis 3:5	
Luke 4:6	

Satan tempts us with promises of POWER. The devil uses the same trick of tempting Jesus with elevated status and authority ("I will give you all their authority and splendor") that he used to convince Adam and Eve that they needed to possess the knowledge of good and evil. Yet Jesus does not reach for power, but instead "he humbled himself" (Philippians 2:8). He trusted fully in God's providence, knowing that God's power would sustain him. He fought against the devil's lies with the truth of God's Holy Scripture.

■ **Question #3**: Look at Luke 4:18-20. Circle all of the verbs in the passage; specifically those words that describe what actions Jesus will take. What has he come to do? List those words here.

God keeps his PROMISES. We saw in Exodus how God kept the promise he made to Moses that he would rescue his people from slavery. But by the time of Isaiah, we find his people in a much deeper kind of slavery: they are trapped in a world where shalom is corrupted. Even more than this, we recognize from these passages that God has a plan to send a savior to restore shalom. He is actively doing things to bring his people rescue, making good on his promise.

■ **Question #4:** Why do you think Jesus quotes Isaiah when he is declaring his mission on earth? Before reading this passage what would you have said that Jesus was sent for? How does the Luke passage support or change that?

Jesus has come to bring real, tangible justice ON EARTH. The book of Isaiah includes many verses that describe God's heart for justice, and when Jesus comes to earth, the first way he introduces himself is by quoting the prophet Isaiah and announcing that he has come to bring "sight to the blind" and "proclaim freedom for prisoners" among other redemptive and restorative acts. These are very real, tangible actions that he proclaims as a significant part of his mission on earth.

Jesus is very specifically linking himself to this savior in Isaiah who will bring justice to the poor. Notice also how clearly he says that this Scripture has been fulfilled *today*. This is amazing encouragement for us to know that when we participate in the work of justice here on earth, we are participating in the work that Jesus made the huge journey from heaven to do. Doing the work of justice is not just good; it is Christlike!

An IJM client stands proudly before her neighbors and family gathered for a "Community Guarantee Meeting," where village members support her application for citizenship rights in Thailand.

||||||||||||||||||||||||||||||||||||||||||||||||||||||||||||||||||||||||||||||||||||||||||||||||||||||||||||||||||||||||||||||||||||||||||||||||

God is all about restoring what was once lost and bringing hope to hopeless situations.

In northern Pakistan lived a young girl named Malala Yousafzai. Malala is a bright young girl who was desperate to get an education, learn and grow to be an intelligent and active woman. Unfortunately, Malala lived in the Swat Valley, a region in Pakistan controlled by the Taliban who do not let women go to school. But Malala and a brave group of girls kept going to school, even as school buildings around them were being destroyed. They knew that this rule was unfair and that something was wrong. Malala would not be silent about her desire for all young girls to get an education, and so she started writing a blog for the BBC about her life under Taliban rule and her desire to promote girls' education.

One day in October 2012, a Taliban gunman came onto the school bus that was taking Malala and some friends home from school. He shot Malala in the head and neck, trying to silence this fifteen-year-old girl. Malala was taken to England, where she received treatment and eventually survived the injury. For her sixteenth birthday, Malala was invited to address a special session of the United Nations. She is the youngest person ever to win a Nobel Peace Prize.

But even more exciting than the story of her recovery is what happened back in her home province. At first, the news of the shooting kept many girls from going to school out of fear for their lives. But aide workers and teachers began to fight the fear, teaching parents about how important it is for their daughters to receive an education. Clearly, what had been intended for evil God was able to turn around for good. Amazingly, the number of girls going to school in nearby villages has increased since Malala was shot. A ten-year-old girl called Tasleem said, "Before Malala was shot we didn't think we should go to school. My mum saw what happened on TV. That made her think. After this she decided her girls should also be in school and should get a good education."[1]

God was at work in Swat Valley to redeem an unjust society where shalom had been broken by lies and inequality. He gave Malala a second chance at life and he gave the girls in the region a second chance at education.

||||||||||||||||||||||||||||||||||||||||||||||||||||||||||||||||||||||||||||||||||||||||||||||||||||||||||||||||||||||||||||||||||||||||||||||||

💡 Review

What insight do the passages from this session give you into Jesus' purpose on earth?

❝❞ Respond

Re-read the Isaiah passage. Similar to the exercise we did with the Luke passage, notice the verbs that you see in these verses. In your life, do you need God to proclaim, release, bestow or comfort? Consider writing a short prayer here, asking God to act.

Using these words as prompts, list some ways that you can act to bring about shalom and justice.

What could I proclaim?

What could I release?

What might I bestow?

How could I comfort?

For Further Reflection

You intended to harm me, but God intended it for good to accomplish what is now being done, the saving of many lives. (Genesis 50:20)

The LORD himself goes before you and will be with you; he will never leave you nor forsake you. (Deuteronomy 31:8)

He is the Maker of heaven and earth,
    the sea, and everything in them—
    he remains faithful forever.
He upholds the cause of the oppressed
    and gives food to the hungry.
The LORD sets prisoners free,
    the LORD gives sight to the blind,
the LORD lifts up those who are bowed down,
    the LORD loves the righteous.
The LORD watches over the foreigner
    and sustains the fatherless and the widow,
        but he frustrates the ways of the wicked. (Psalm 146:6-9)

An IJM lawyer presents a case before a judge in Rwanda.

AFRICA—KENYA

JOSEPH'S STORY

When a riot broke out near the small shop Joseph ran in a popular marketplace, he walked outside to investigate the commotion. Joseph was struck by a stray bullet fired by police in an attempt to control the crowd.

Joseph

It was December 2010, and it was the beginning of a nightmare for Joseph and his family.

The same police who accidently shot him later ordered him arrested, fabricating the charge that Joseph had injured the police and stolen their weapons. He was thrown in prison and charged with robbery with violence—a capital offense. Joseph, an innocent man and father of six, knew he had done nothing wrong. He had been in the wrong place at the wrong time, but he was helpless to defend himself and could not afford a lawyer.

IJM Kenya learned of the charges against this innocent man and began representing him before the Nairobi court. The trial dragged on for months despite the obvious lack of evidence against Joseph. His imprisonment left his wife and six children without the support of their primary breadwinner.

The frequent delays in the trial left Joseph's wife distraught. She gave birth to their sixth child in the first months that Joseph was in prison. She was too poor to make regular visits, and months passed as the trial stalled. Every delay compounded her anxiety for Joseph and their future together.

When IJM staff showed up at the courtroom on May 3, 2012, for Joseph's final hearing, the power was out. Determined that this should not cause yet another delay, IJM attorney Christine Nknoge ran across the street to purchase candles.

The judge read the verdict by candlelight: Joseph was declared innocent.

"Our team in Kenya is in full celebration mode right now," said IJM Kenya's field office director, Shawn Kohl. "Joseph's wife and his children will get to see their dad after over a year. We will keep walking with this family to restore all that has been lost, but today we rejoice that Joseph is free at last."

Learn more and see a video about Joseph at ijm.org/josephs-story.

7

Pictures of
the Kingdom of God

Often it can be tempting to relegate Jesus to the spiritual things in life. He's in charge of forgiving sins, grace and sanctification (or insert some other "churchy" concept). But when it comes to the nitty-gritty of life, does Jesus really understand? Does he understand what it is like to look for a job? To be in need of housing? Does he know loneliness or boredom? He seems so godlike and so "of heaven."

But in this next session, we see a picture of Jesus, a flesh-and-blood Jesus, walking in and among the people, meeting people where they are. He is up close and personal to the sick, to the lame. This is a Jesus who has to eat because he has a body. This is a picture of God, the God who comes near. We see a picture of Jesus, who feels compassion and anger. This is not some automaton Jesus, who feels nothing, is surprised by nothing. We begin to see pictures of Jesus who cares not just about people's souls, but about their bodies and their everyday reality too.

Recall

Last session we discussed God's desire to build his kingdom for justice on earth. What did Jesus clarify as the reasons he was sent?

In what ways are you tempted to go to God with *only* spiritual things? When it comes to other areas of your life, why do you think Jesus isn't your first choice for advice?

⌻ Read

John 5:1-9

[1]Some time later, Jesus went up to Jerusalem for one of the Jewish festivals. [2]Now there is in Jerusalem near the Sheep Gate a pool, which in Aramaic is called Bethesda and which is surrounded by five covered colonnades. [3]Here a great number of disabled people used to lie—the blind, the lame, the paralyzed. [5]One who was there had been an invalid for thirty-eight years. [6]When Jesus saw him lying there and learned that he had been in this condition for a long time, he asked him, "Do you want to get well?"

[7]"Sir," the invalid replied, "I have no one to help me into the pool when the water is stirred. While I am trying to get in, someone else goes down ahead of me."

[8]Then Jesus said to him, "Get up! Pick up your mat and walk." [9]At once the man was cured; he picked up his mat and walked.

Luke 14:1-6

[1]One Sabbath, when Jesus went to eat in the house of a prominent Pharisee, he was being carefully watched. [2]There in front of him was a man suffering from abnormal swelling of his body. [3]Jesus asked the Pharisees and experts in the law, "Is it lawful to heal on the Sabbath or not?" [4]But they remained silent. So taking hold of the man, he healed him and sent him on his way.

[5]Then he asked them, "If one of you has a child or an ox that falls into a well on the Sabbath day, will you not immediately pull it out?" [6]And they had nothing to say.

Matthew 14:13-21

[13]When Jesus heard what had happened, he withdrew by boat privately to a solitary place. Hearing of this, the crowds followed him on foot from the towns. [14]When Jesus landed and saw a large crowd, he had compassion on them and healed their sick.

[15]As evening approached, the disciples came to him and said, "This is a remote place, and it's already getting late. Send the crowds away, so they can go to the villages and buy themselves some food."

[16]Jesus replied, "They do not need to go away. You give them something to eat."

[17]"We have here only five loaves of bread and two fish," they answered.

[18]"Bring them here to me," he said. [19]And he directed the people to sit down on the grass. Taking the five loaves and the two fish and looking up to heaven, he gave thanks and broke the loaves. Then he gave them to the disciples, and the disciples gave them to the people. [20]They all ate and were satisfied, and the disciples picked up twelve basketfuls of broken pieces that were left over. [21]The number of those who ate was about five thousand men, besides women and children.

Q Reflect

■ **Question #1:** What do you notice about Jesus' response in each of these three situations? Record your observations below.

John passage:

Luke passage:

Matthew passage:

■ **Question #2:** How do these three stories connect to Jesus' statement from Luke 4:18-19?

Justice means SEEING people as God sees them. In all of these stories, we see Jesus interacting with the poor. We learn the man by the pool had been cast out by his community for thirty-eight years. He was discouraged and cast aside even by others who were in desperate positions. Most people probably wouldn't even have noticed him. But Jesus saw this man through God's eyes. Jesus saw a child of God, made in his image. He saw a human being full of value, dignity and faith.

In the second story, Jesus tells the Pharisees to think about people in need as if they were members of their household: "If one of you has a child or an ox that falls into a well on the Sabbath day, will you not immediately pull it out?" Similarly, in the story of the feeding of the five thousand, Jesus saw the crowd of thousands who needed healing and "had compassion on them." He saw them as precious people God had made.

If we are to follow in the footsteps of Jesus and love people as Jesus loved them, we also need to be able to recognize them through God's eyes, as people extremely precious, valuable and loved by their Creator. We must not see people as society sees them, but as Jesus sees them.

■ **Question #3**: Who are the people who are viewed as "the least of these" in your community or society? What social barriers make it difficult for people in your community to help those in need?

Doing justice often means bravely DEFYING social norms. In order to do the work of justice and to bring about the kingdom of God, Jesus had to break through the social and cultural barriers that kept people from helping their neighbors. For example, the Pharisees promoted the attitude that following the law was more valuable than the lives of people. In order to heal the man in desperate need of care, Jesus had to deal with social opposition.

Jesus did not let social customs prevent him from reaching out to this man even though most others would not have associated with him. With Jesus' example, we learn something about what it means to do justice and to build the kingdom of God. In order to truly break the chains of injustice, we need to put people before social norms and before our own reputations, just like Jesus did.

A vigil for child sexual assault victims is held in Bolivia.

Jesus was widely criticized for helping people because he reached out to those who society saw as worthless, or because he acted in ways that went against the culture of the day. In order to be more like Christ, we need to be equally brave and learn to see people as more important than anything else.

During the Bosnian War of 1992–1995, the Serbian and Bosnian people groups living in Yugoslavia were embroiled in a brutal battle for land, which was perpetuated by religious and ethnic prejudices. The Serbs were predominantly Christian, while the Bosnians were predominantly Muslim. These differences, on top of years of fighting, had made each group hate the other to the point of killing each other. An American journalist, Chris Hedges, was covering the war, and while he was living in Bosnia, he heard a story of a Serbian Christian family living in an area populated mostly by Bosnian Muslims. This family had refused to take part in ethnic cleansing and so they were ostracized by their own people. Both of their sons died. One was killed in a car crash and one was taken by Muslim police and disappeared. Five months later, the mother gave birth to a baby girl but she was unable to nurse the child. Severe food shortages meant that children and the elderly were dying in droves. The only thing the family had to feed the baby was tea. Only five days old, she was dying. But on the fifth day, a man arrived before dawn with half a liter of milk for the child. The neighbor was a Bosnian Muslim who had one cow, which he kept outside the city so it wouldn't get killed by Serbian sniper fire. The only time he could milk it without getting shot was at night. This neighbor came back the next morning, and the next, and the next. His friends started to insult him. They told him to save his milk for Muslim children and let the Serbian children die. But the man came back every day for 442 days, until the family was able to leave for Serbia. He refused to take any money from the family.

Hedges writes that although the couple said they could never forgive those who had taken their son, they could not listen to other Serbs talking ill of Muslims without telling this story.[1]

Review

How does the Muslim man in this story live out the three lessons learned this week?

❝❞ Respond

What are some examples of ways that our actions can point to a God who cares about the physical as well as the spiritual needs of a person? Similarly to the child who offered his lunch for the five thousand, we are asked to simply bring what we have to God for his use. Consider your time, skills, passions, job, community. What might you offer to God so that you can care for others? How could he multiply what you offer?

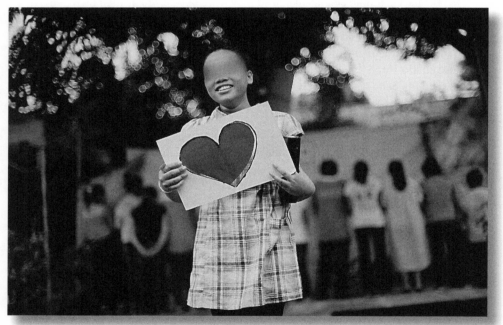

A client who was rescued from sex trafficking by IJM shares the artwork she's drawn during an event at an aftercare home, where she will find restoration.

For Further Reflection

As you go, proclaim this message: "The kingdom of heaven has come near." Heal the sick, raise the dead, cleanse those who have leprosy, drive out demons. Freely you have received; freely give. (Matthew 10:7-8)

The King will reply, "Truly I tell you, whatever you did for one of the least of these brothers and sisters of mine, you did for me." (Matthew 25:40)

The thief comes only to steal and kill and destroy; I have come that you may have life, and have it to the full. (John 10:10)

Very truly I tell you, whoever believes in me will do the works I have been doing, and they will do even greater things than these, because I am going to the Father. (John 14:12)

8

Justice and
the Cross of Christ

The cross is many things to many people today. To some it is an ornament around the neck, and to others it is a relic of immense spiritual significance. Some have it on their clothes, while others hang it in their cars and homes. Some consider it very casually, while others would ascribe great reverence to it. In the first century, the cross would have been rare, as it depicted a particularly painful and barbaric method of public execution. But today it adorns the walls of churches and chapels around the world, from the most modern cities to the most rural villages. When I (Abraham) travel to different countries one of my favorite things to do is to look at the different types of crosses—each with its own cultural and historic influences. If you did an internet search of the word "cross" you'd come up with thousands of unique images.

What is undeniable, however, is the centrality of the cross to Christianity. It is the very heart of the gospel and the supreme demonstration of the love God has for sinful humanity. Crucifixion was the ultimate degradation and humiliation, yet Jesus' death on the cross has eternal and cosmic significance. It forms the very core of Christian theology and worldview.

This session will allow us to reflect on what the cross teaches us about God's heart for the poor and the oppressed. As we look at the abuse and oppression in our neighborhoods and communities, are there things we can learn from the cross? Today we'll discuss the crucifixion of Christ and how it compels us toward the work of justice.

⤴ Recall

During the previous sessions, we've talked about how God prioritizes justice and brings justice to those in need through the brave and small acts of people like us. How are you beginning to think about being a "carrier of justice" to those who need it?

⌐ Read

Luke 23:13-49

¹³Pilate called together the chief priests, the rulers and the people, ¹⁴and said to them, "You brought me this man as one who was inciting the people to rebellion. I have examined him in your presence and have found no basis for your charges against him. ¹⁵Neither has Herod, for he sent him back to us; as you can see, he has done nothing to deserve death. ¹⁶Therefore, I will punish him and then release him."

¹⁸But the whole crowd shouted, "Away with this man! Release Barabbas to us!" ¹⁹(Barabbas had been thrown into prison for an insurrection in the city, and for murder.)

²⁰Wanting to release Jesus, Pilate appealed to them again. ²¹But they kept shouting, "Crucify him! Crucify him!"

²²For the third time he spoke to them: "Why? What crime has this man committed? I have found in him no grounds for the death penalty. Therefore I will have him punished and then release him."

²³But with loud shouts they insistently demanded that he be crucified, and their shouts prevailed. ²⁴So Pilate decided to grant their demand. ²⁵He released the man who had been thrown into prison for insurrection and murder, the one they asked for, and surrendered Jesus to their will.

²⁶As the soldiers led him away, they seized Simon from Cyrene, who was on his way in from the country, and put the cross on him and made him carry it behind Jesus. ²⁷A large number of people followed him, including women who mourned and wailed for him. ²⁸Jesus turned and said to them, "Daughters of Jerusalem, do not weep for me; weep for yourselves and for your children. ²⁹For the time will come when you will say, 'Blessed are the childless women, the wombs that never bore and the breasts that never nursed!' ³⁰Then

> "'they will say to the mountains, "Fall on us!"
> and to the hills, "Cover us!"'

³¹For if people do these things when the tree is green, what will happen when it is dry?"

³²Two other men, both criminals, were also led out with him to be executed. ³³When they came to the place called the Skull, they crucified him there, along with the criminals—one on his right, the other on his left. ³⁴Jesus said, "Father, forgive them, for they do not know what they are doing." And they divided up his clothes by casting lots.

³⁵The people stood watching, and the rulers even sneered at him. They said, "He saved others; let him save himself if he is God's Messiah, the Chosen One."

³⁶The soldiers also came up and mocked him. They offered him wine vinegar ³⁷and said, "If you are the king of the Jews, save yourself."

³⁸There was a written notice above him, which read: THIS IS THE KING OF THE JEWS.

³⁹One of the criminals who hung there hurled insults at him: "Aren't you the Messiah? Save yourself and us!"

[40]But the other criminal rebuked him. "Don't you fear God," he said, "since you are under the same sentence? [41]We are punished justly, for we are getting what our deeds deserve. But this man has done nothing wrong."

[42]Then he said, "Jesus, remember me when you come into your kingdom."

[43]Jesus answered him, "Truly I tell you, today you will be with me in paradise."

[44]It was now about noon, and darkness came over the whole land until three in the afternoon, [45]for the sun stopped shining. And the curtain of the temple was torn in two. [46]Jesus called out with a loud voice, "Father, into your hands I commit my spirit." When he had said this, he breathed his last.

[47]The centurion, seeing what had happened, praised God and said, "Surely this was a righteous man." [48]When all the people who had gathered to witness this sight saw what took place, they beat their breasts and went away. [49]But all those who knew him, including the women who had followed him from Galilee, stood at a distance, watching these things.

Reflect

■ **Question #1**: Begin by making a list of adjectives that describe or characterize the scenes in this passage. How would you describe the way in which Jesus died? What words describe the scene, the treatment of Christ and the way in which he received his own death?

As you review your list, try to view it through the lens of justice. What is just about the cross of Christ? What is unjust about it? Complete the chart below, listing your thoughts in either column.

Just	Unjust

Before reading further, spend some time considering this question: What does the crucifixion of Jesus teach us about God's view of justice?

The cross of Christ ASSURES us of God's heart for justice. In this story of Jesus' death on the cross, we start to get a sense of the *huge* price God is willing to pay to restore shalom. Though the death of Christ is a deep injustice, this death opened a path for reconciliation with God, the foundation of a just life.

The weight of our sin and God's inability to condone sin meant that we would have been separated from God for eternity with no way back to shalom. But God so desired to renew his creation and bring back justice to a broken world that he gave his beloved son to bear the enormous weight of that sin, to take the punishment for our sins so that we could be right before God.

Whenever we start to doubt God's heart for justice, we can look at the cross and remember what God gave to restore shalom to this broken world.

■ **Question #2:** How does the cross give you confidence?

IJM staff train police officers in Uganda, equipping them to protect orphans and widows from land theft.

The cross of Christ gives us the HOPE that we need to do the work of justice. The cross of Christ is the best picture we have of God's power to transform lives and rescue his people. This is the moment when the tide of justice turns. God is "making everything new" (Revelation 21:5)!

When we experience setbacks, hardships or difficulties and when we stumble in the work of justice, we can know that these are only temporary obstacles. God has already mapped out a path back to shalom through Jesus Christ so we need not fear that we will fail in this work. The cross of Christ teaches us that justice has ultimately won, so no matter how long it takes we know that when God invites us to do justice with him, we are already part of a successful mission!

Grace, an IJM client in Uganda, sits in her home, which was restored to her by IJM and local officials. Because Grace has land, she can provide food for her children. Because she has a home, she can protect them. And because she has hope, she can teach them to dream.

■ **Question #3:** How might hope provide the fuel you need to face challenging situations of brokenness?

The cross of Christ gives us the HUMILITY we need to do the work of justice. The cross of Christ shows us a picture of ultimate humility. As Jesus is being beaten, scorned and mocked, he keeps his eyes fixed on his goal and restrains his power, demonstrating humility. The cross of Christ is also a humbling moment for us as Christians. We are utterly unable to save ourselves, but we desperately need Jesus to rescue us. This makes us confident of God's great and infinite love for us and at the same time reminds us of how imperfect we would be without Christ. This deep, personal understanding of grace makes it possible for us to go out into the world and help those who we see struggling, trapped or lost, regardless of what we get in return.

The cross gives us the humility we need to help anyone, despite their situation. There was no one too sinful, too poor, too uneducated, too socially estranged or too difficult for Jesus to save, and neither should there be for us. When we understand that we were just as lost and estranged as the people we see suffering around us, it gives us the gratitude and humility to do the work of justice, helping people as Jesus did.

Maximilian Kolbe was a Polish monk of the Franciscan Order. He had worked as a Catholic journalist in Poland and then went to Japan as a missionary for six years. There he founded a monastery in Nagasaki.

During World War II, Kolbe provided shelter to two thousand Jews he hid from the Nazis in the monastery. In February 1941, Kolbe was arrested by the Nazis and taken to Auschwitz as a prisoner.

At the end of July 1941, three prisoners disappeared from the camp. In order to deter others from escaping, the Nazi prison guards picked ten people to be sent to an underground bunker where they would be starved to death. As the Nazis were going through the people picking out the selected ten, one of the men they chose cried out, "My wife! My children!" Since Kolbe had no family he volunteered to be sent in the man's place out of mercy for him and his family.

In this underground prison, Kolbe celebrated Mass each day with the other prisoners. He led them in song and prayer and encouraged the others that they would soon be in heaven. After two weeks of starvation and dehydration, Kolbe was the last one of the prisoners alive. Eventually, the Nazis killed him with a lethal injection.

The prisoner whose place he took, Franciszek Gajowniczek, survived life in Auschwitz, was liberated at the end of the war and reunited with his wife, Helena. He lived until he was ninety-four years old.[1]

Review

How might you explain the fact that the cross embodies injustice and justice at the same time?

❝❝ Respond

Which of these three points has the most impact on you as you think about doing the work and ministry of justice? Why?

- The assurance that justice is a component of God's character
- The hope that God provides a path back to the restoration of shalom
- The humility that results from our true understanding of Christ's cross: when we realize our deep need for grace, we are better able to extend grace to others

Take a moment to write a short prayer to God. Reflect on what you're feeling about his crucifixion and ask for the assurance, the hope or the humility that you need.

For Further Reflection

The greatest among you will be your servant. (Matthew 23:11)

This is how we know what love is: Jesus Christ laid down his life for us. And we ought to lay down our lives for our brothers and sisters. If anyone has material possessions and sees a brother or sister in need but has no pity on them, how can the love of God be in that person? (1 John 3:16-17)

We love because he first loved us. (1 John 4:19)

The Church and Justice

I (Nikki) was once challenged with this question: If someone were to remove all the things you say about your faith and the overtly religious things you do (attend church, pray, etc.) would there be enough evidence in your lifestyle to convict you in court that you are a Christian?

I thought about that. I looked at my budget and my receipts to see how I spent my money. I looked at my calendar and removed items like "Bible study" and wondered if my faith affected how I spent my time and with whom I met. What do my choices say about what I believe and what I value? Is there something in there that is so unusual that the only explanation for the evidence is "She must be a Christian?"

A picture of the radical community of the early church in Acts became a model for my group of friends in college. Could we also be so committed to God's people that it would affect our daily life, how we used our possessions and who we hung out with?

Folks tried creative living arrangements so that rooms could be opened up as common rooms. At one point, six of us slept in a dorm room meant for two so that we would have a communal room that could be a place of ministry for the dorm. That first morning, it was tough when all the different alarm clocks went off at different times! But it was exciting to try to use the little that we had to actually live out what we believed.

I still think about that challenge when I make major life decisions. Does the movie of my life make sense? Do my choices in my career, living situations, finances and relationships make logical sense apart from God? Or are there some truly risky things, like radical acts of love or sacrifice, that could only point to the existence of a God who is present and working in our world today? This session leads us to reflect on a similar question for each of our lives.

⤷ Recall

In the last session, we discussed how the cross of Christ inspired us to do the work of justice, personally and in the church. We asked for assurance, hope and humility. As you think about your local church community, how well are you doing at participating in the ministry of justice? Would you like to see yourself doing more? Would you like to see your church do more?

⌷ Read

Acts 2:42–3:10

[42]They devoted themselves to the apostles' teaching and to fellowship, to the breaking of bread and to prayer. [43]Everyone was filled with awe at the many wonders and signs performed by the apostles. [44]All the believers were together and had everything in common. [45]They sold property and possessions to give to anyone who had need. [46]Every day they continued to meet together in the temple courts. They broke bread in their homes and ate together with glad and sincere hearts, [47]praising God and enjoying the favor of all the people. And the Lord added to their number daily those who were being saved.

3 One day Peter and John were going up to the temple at the time of prayer—at three in the afternoon. [2]Now a man who was lame from birth was being carried to the temple gate called Beautiful, where he was put every day to beg from those going into the temple courts. [3]When he saw Peter and John about to enter, he asked them for money. [4]Peter looked straight at him, as did John. Then Peter said, "Look at us!" [5]So the man gave them his attention, expecting to get something from them.

[6]Then Peter said, "Silver or gold I do not have, but what I do have I give you. In the name of Jesus Christ of Nazareth, walk." [7]Taking him by the right hand, he helped him up, and instantly the man's feet and ankles became strong. [8]He jumped to his feet and began to walk. Then he went with them into the temple courts, walking and jumping, and praising God. [9]When all the people saw him walking and praising God, [10]they recognized him as the same man who used to sit begging at the temple gate called Beautiful, and they were filled with wonder and amazement at what had happened to him.

🔍 Reflect

In this passage we see the early church fulfilling their call to be the "hands and feet" of Jesus Christ after he has ascended into heaven.

■ **Question #1:** What specific actions or practices do you see in this passage that indicate the early church behaved in culturally risky, brave or sacrificial ways?

What verses indicate the source of the strength and passion in the early church? List them below.

Now, consider the relationship between the source of power for the early church, the actions and practices of the early church, and the resulting fruit of ministry in the early church. Complete the flow chart below. Are the actions more evangelistic or justice focused? What would happen if one of the components in this sequence was removed?

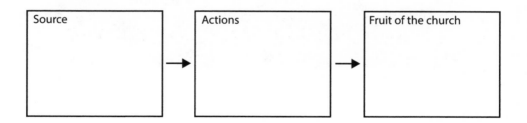

Source		Actions		Fruit of the church

■ **Question #2:** Consider the relationship between justice and evangelism. Re-read Acts 3:8-10. What is the result of the transformation in this man's life? In the life of others?

The work of JUSTICE and EVANGELISM are paired together in building God's kingdom. In Acts 2, we get a picture of the early church sharing everything "in common" and paying close attention to the needs of those around them. The Scripture says that their generous and grateful attitudes were noticed by the people around them, who had "favor" with them. This picture of a just society was infectious, and people noticed the beautiful shalom that was present in this community to the extent that "the Lord added to their number day by day."

In the same way, when Peter and John heal the lame man in Acts 3, they are doing justice to a man who, because of his health, has been forgotten by his society and has not been allowed to work, have a family or be a part of society.

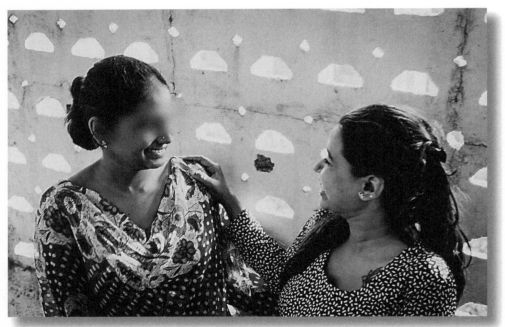

An IJM client rescued from sex trafficking laughs with her social worker in India.

This act of justice has a ripple effect as we are told that those who witnessed the transformation in this man's life, both physical and spiritual, "were filled with wonder and amazement," probably asking themselves, "Who is this God who heals the oppressed and restores joy?"

Within the Christian community, heavy emphasis is placed on preaching the gospel, leading Bible studies or evangelizing our non-believing friends. We can tend to think of the work of justice as secondary or an add-on. But the Bible makes it clear that evangelism can be carried out through the work of justice. When we respond to the deep needs of others, we are demonstrating to them that God is good and loving. This is not to say that we should do justice in order to convert people, nor should we set aside preaching the gospel in favor of justice. No, we should do the work of God as Jesus did, seeing justice and evangelism as complimentary to one another. As God's "hands and feet," the church is continuing the work of justice that Jesus started.

▪ **Question #3**: Based on this passage, what are the qualities of people who are used by God?

The people of the early church lived out justice in their DAILY lives and in their EXTRAORDINARY activities. In the first passage, we get a picture of the day-to-day life of the early church, what their community was like and how they used their resources. The early church found a way to live out justice in their daily lives. This passage in Acts describes very clearly that the early church was economically just since resources were used for the good of those who most needed them instead of out of greediness or hoarding.

Elsewhere in Acts and in Paul's letters, we learn that the church was widely known for breaking social boundaries. Slaves and freemen, widows, Jews and Gentiles, men and women would all eat and commune together. God's justice proclaims that every member of the community is considered equal in his sight.

▪ **Question #4**: Based on this passage, what was essential for the work of the early church to thrive?

The church can only do justice with God's POWER. From Acts, we learn how much the church relies on God's power and the person of Jesus Christ in order to be able to do justice. In Acts 3, Peter and John make it clear that they can only work miracles and restore a lame man's life through the power of Jesus Christ. It was not Peter or John that had the power to heal this man, but Jesus. Notice that when the man is healed, he praises God! Without faith in God's power, Peter and John could have never healed the man.

In the same way, we learn from Acts 2 that the early church was continually "praising God." Where do you think they got the strength and trust to surrender all of their earthly goods and security to others? Knowing that they could trust

God for everything they needed gave the church members the strength to live such a radical and courageous life of trusting in God and in one another.

||||||||||||||||||||||||||||||||||||||||||||||||||||||||||||||||||||||||||||||||||||||||||||||||||||||||||||||||||||||||||||||||||||||||||||||||||||||||||||||||||||

During her ministry, Mother Teresa often struggled to find places to house the dying poor that she was called to care for. There were very few options, so the local authorities offered her a space in the temple of the Hindu goddess Kali. This space had been intended to house pilgrims but had evolved into a hangout for thieves, drug addicts and pimps. Word got out in the city that a Christian woman was misusing the temple by using it as a place to convert people away from their traditional Hindu beliefs. The public protested at city hall, demanding that Mother Teresa be evicted. The police commissioner agreed, but stated that he would personally check the site first to make sure for himself that the allegations were true.

The police commissioner went to visit Mother Teresa's site in the temple. He met her as she was caring for a poor, destitute man, putting potassium permanganate on his worm-infested wound. The stench was unbearable. Mother Teresa invited the commissioner in and showed him around. When he came out of the temple to meet the crowd that had formed outside, he said, "I gave you my word that I would throw this woman out of here, and I would like to keep it. But, before I do, you will have to get your mothers and sisters to do what she does. I make that the only condition for exercising my authority."

This angry crowd had hardened their hearts against hearing the teachings of Jesus to the point where they were not at all willing to hear the good news of Christ. Evangelism would have been futile. But this crowd and the police commissioner could not harden their hearts against the selfless works of a woman who understood what justice meant and acted it out without question. Mother Teresa performed her role as the "hands and feet" of Christ, and by doing so gave a much more powerful message of the gospel by *showing* people the love of Christ instead of just telling them.[1]

||||||||||||||||||||||||||||||||||||||||||||||||||||||||||||||||||||||||||||||||||||||||||||||||||||||||||||||||||||||||||||||||||||||||||||||||||||||||||||||||||||

💡 Review

If we were to speak with someone from the early church today, what might they have to say about the ways our churches engage in justice and evangelism? What would they find to be positive? What would they find was missing or negative?

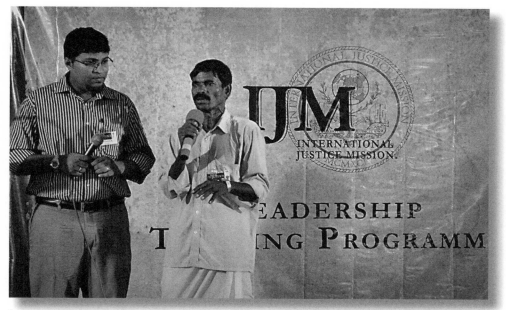

Raman, an IJM client and former slave who is now living in freedom as a leader in his community, presents an IJM leadership training session.

❞❞ Respond

The life of Mother Teresa challenges us to prioritize the ministry of justice in our own lives. Begin to think about how you might increase the ministry of justice in your own life and church. Write down two to three things that you can do, even this week, to work for justice for another person. Consider your community, family, work environment, current church ministries, etc.

For Further Reflection

But when they were oppressed they cried out to you. From heaven you heard them, and in your great compassion you gave them deliverers, who rescued them from the hand of their enemies. (Nehemiah 9:27)

Whoever oppresses the poor shows contempt for their Maker,
    but whoever is kind to the needy honors God. (Proverbs 14:31)

In everything I did, I showed you that by this kind of hard work we must help the weak, remembering the words the Lord Jesus himself said: "It is more blessed to give than to receive." (Acts 20:35)

10

Pleading for Justice

One of the questions pastors often get asked about prayer goes something like this: "Pastor, God is sovereign and omnipotent and omnipresent and all that, right? Which means he knows everything and he can do everything and he is present everywhere, right? So if that is true, why do we really need to pray? He already knows everything without us telling him! Right?"

Sound familiar?

As the parent of a teenager and a preteen, I (Abraham) am eager to respond to the "why" question by saying, "Because God said so!" In Matthew 6:8, Jesus says, "Your Father knows what you need before you ask him," but Jesus still commands us to pray.

This is true! But I think John Calvin offers another perspective on why we must pray in light of God's sovereignty: "It was not so much for God's good, as it was for our good." He adds that the fruit of the practice of prayer is "that our hearts may be fired with a zealous and burning desire ever to seek, love, and serve God."[1]

As you think about your own engagement with the poor and the oppressed in your community, it is our hope that this session will allow you to think about the usefulness of prayer in your work.

Why pray?

We hope this session will help you answer that question.

 Recall

Last session we discussed our need for God's power to do the work of justice in our daily lives and in our communities. How is prayer connected to the power of God?

⌸ Read

Luke 18:1-8

[1]Then Jesus told his disciples a parable to show them that they should always pray and not give up. [2]He said: "In a certain town there was a judge who neither feared God nor cared what people thought. [3]And there was a widow in that town who kept coming to him with the plea, 'Grant me justice against my adversary.'

[4]"For some time he refused. But finally he said to himself, 'Even though I don't fear God or care what people think, [5]yet because this widow keeps bothering me, I will see that she gets justice, so that she won't eventually come and attack me!'"

[6]And the Lord said, "Listen to what the unjust judge says. [7]And will not God bring about justice for his chosen ones, who cry out to him day and night? Will he keep putting them off ? [8]I tell you, he will see that they get justice, and quickly. However, when the Son of Man comes, will he find faith on the earth?"

Matthew 6:9-13

[9]"This, then, is how you should pray:

"'Our Father in heaven,
hallowed be your name,
[10]your kingdom come,
your will be done,
    on earth as it is in heaven.
[11]Give us today our daily bread.
[12]And forgive us our debts,
    as we also have forgiven our debtors.
[13]And lead us not into temptation,
    but deliver us from the evil one.'"

⌕ Reflect

■ **Question #1:** When you consider the work of justice, how often do you consider prayer an integral part of that work? Why do you think that is?

Prayer is ESSENTIAL to the work of justice. The first passage is best known as a parable about how eager God is to listen to our prayers and answer them, but it also describes very well the reality of pleading for justice. Just like the widow in this passage, we are most often on the weak side of power. We ourselves do not have the ability, the training or the high rank to make decisions or create laws that will protect the poor.

Sometimes, like this widow, all we have is a voice to plead with. But as this parable tells us, this voice is *powerful*. As Christians, our responsibility is to plead with God on behalf of those who are oppressed that he—in his infinite power—will work in the hearts and minds of the perpetrators and the law enforcement officials.

■ **Question #2:** What is the relationship between prayer and perseverance? Read Luke 18:7 again. How frequently are those who seek justice praying to God?

Margaret, an IJM client who was sexually assaulted, throws a soccer ball with her family.

We should pray FAITHFULLY and PERSISTENTLY. This story is all about the power of petition to make change, especially when we have a God who cares so deeply for us and the people we pray for. If even a stubborn and hardhearted judge will eventually give in to the petition of a widow, how much more will God do what we ask of him? This parable should encourage us that God is listening to our prayers and will answer them according to his wisdom, even if it doesn't happen immediately.

- **Question #3:** What examples of humility do you see in these two passages?

Prayer teaches us to RELY on God. As a people who seek to bring shalom to this world, we must remember that this is not *our* mission, but *God's* mission. An important part of praying to God is acknowledging that he is the one who is sovereign—he is in control of everything. Part of praying is the act of submitting yourself to the will of God.

When Jesus teaches his disciples how to pray, an important part of that prayer is, "Your will be done, on earth as it is in heaven." When we align our will with God's will, amazing things can happen!

When we pray, we admit that we can't solve these problems with our own strength, but that we rely on God's strength. In this way, prayer not only transforms the lives we pray about, but it also transforms our hearts as we learn to trust that God is ultimately in control and works all things "for the good of those who love him" (Romans 8:28).

For eighteen months Michael sat in a Kenyan prison cell condemned to die for a crime he did not commit. He had been convicted of robbery with violence connected to the murder of a UN security officer. The judge and the police pressed false charges against Michael because in Kenya, the government practices a very "results-oriented justice" model: someone (it doesn't matter who) must pay for every crime. This someone was Michael.

IJM attorneys heard of Michael's case in 2010 and worked to push the case through to trial, confident that it would result in freedom. IJM staff prayed and wept for Michael's case. They also brought his story to IJM's Global Prayer Gathering held each spring in Washington, DC. Hundreds prayed for Michael to be released from his unfair imprisonment.

Six weeks after the Global Prayer Gathering, Michael was released on bail. The High Court granted bail to a convict—not just any convict, but a death row inmate convicted of a robbery that resulted in the murder of a prominent citizen. Such a request had never been granted in the entire history of Kenya. This request was granted just weeks after the request was fervently lifted up in prayer. God responded, for he hears the pleas of his people and does the inconceivable to grant freedom.[2]

Michael, who was falsely charged and detained in Kenya, celebrates his freedom while walking out of prison after IJM pled his case and secured his release.

Review

Why does God encourage us to pray with perseverance and humility? What do we learn about God and his character through prayer?

Respond

In the passage in Luke, we read that the widow kept coming to the judge with a plea. Are we deeply enough concerned with the need for justice that we are pleading for it? Consider the ways that you could change your practice of prayer to include more humble or urgent requests for people in need of justice. Below are two suggested ways that you can enter into prayer for the work of justice. Select one and spend some time in prayer as you're closing this session. Consider including this rhythm of prayer daily in your life.

Suggestion 1: Pray for the following:

• *Wisdom*: Pray that God will give you wisdom as you think about and encounter injustice. Pray that he would wisely show you what is true.

- *Love*: Ask God to cultivate love for people who are far away, unfamiliar or unlike you.

- *Hope*: Pray against the temptation to despair in the face of injustice.

- *Guidance*: Pray for people that may help and guide you as you seek to do God's work of justice.

Suggestion 2: Use the ACTS model to guide your time in prayer as you sit in the presence of God.

A–Adoration: *Express your love and worship to God.*

C–Confession: *Confess your sins, repent and ask for his forgiveness.*

T–Thanksgiving: *Praise him for his faithfulness, for his goodness and for his love.*

S–Supplication: *Make your requests known to God. He loves to give his children good gifts.*

For Further Reflection

> The LORD said, "I have indeed seen the misery of my people in Egypt. I have heard them crying out because of their slave drivers, and I am concerned about their suffering." (Exodus 3:7)

> If you remain in me and my words remain in you, ask whatever you wish, and it will be done for you. (John 15:7)

> Do not be anxious about anything, but in every situation, by prayer and petition, with thanksgiving, present your requests to God. And the peace of God, which transcends all understanding, will guard your hearts and minds in Christ Jesus. (Philippians 4:6-7)

> The prayer of a righteous person is powerful and effective. (James 5:16)

11

Surveying the Wreckage

In the beginning of my justice awakening, I (Nikki) took a team of young adults to various communities at the margins to learn about what God was doing there through local people. We went on a three-city poverty immersion, living in the local slums with only fifteen dollars in our pocket for the summer. During the day we worked at local churches, ministries or community organizations. In between, we would study Scripture and learn from local teachers. But I remember there was one day that changed everything for our group.

We were visiting the third and final city on our summer trip—Bangkok. We had lived in the slums in Nairobi, the garbage village in Cairo and now were staying at a church on the edge of the slums in Bangkok. The issues we were seeing were intense—we went out in the evenings into the red-light districts to help a local outreach ministry. Seeing the sale of girls for tourists from every country shook me. And I think it was the first time I experienced anger at injustice.

Our conversations were full of debate and questions about what was happening. And to be honest we jumped to quick conclusions about how to "solve" the problems. But a visit to the International Red Cross and the United Nations reoriented our group. We came in passionate about quick change. But we learned so much from these people who had been working in the country and in these communities for a long time. We learned about the economic factors that created a pipeline of girls willing to take large risks for jobs. We learned about cultural factors and the value of one gender over another. We learned about the spiritual background of the country and the ways those values manifest in society. Additionally, the political environment and military environment contribute in complex ways. We were humbled when we saw that the justice issues around us had a complex history and evolution.

But it also made the work that God was doing more hope-filled. We saw God moving in women's lives, in the sex industry, through churches and ministries. The reality was both more terrible and more hopeful than we ever imagined.

⌕ Recall

Last session we discussed how powerful our prayers are in persevering in the work of justice. In order to persevere, we should have an understanding of the injustice that we'll encounter. How might your eyes be opening to injustice around you that you might have overlooked before these discussions?

⌕ Read

Nehemiah 1:1-11; 2:11-18

[1]The words of Nehemiah son of Hakaliah:

In the month of Kislev in the twentieth year, while I was in the citadel of Susa, [2]Hanani, one of my brothers, came from Judah with some other men, and I questioned them about the Jewish remnant that had survived the exile, and also about Jerusalem.

[3]They said to me, "Those who survived the exile and are back in the province are in great trouble and disgrace. The wall of Jerusalem is broken down, and its gates have been burned with fire."

[4]When I heard these things, I sat down and wept. For some days I mourned and fasted and prayed before the God of heaven. [5]Then I said:

"LORD, the God of heaven, the great and awesome God, who keeps his covenant of love with those who love him and keep his commandments, [6]let your ear be attentive and your eyes open to hear the prayer your servant is praying before you day and night for your servants, the people of Israel. I confess the sins we Israelites, including myself and my father's family, have committed against you. [7]We have acted very wickedly toward you. We have not obeyed the commands, decrees and laws you gave your servant Moses.

[8]"Remember the instruction you gave your servant Moses, saying, 'If you are unfaithful, I will scatter you among the nations, [9]but if you return to me and obey my commands, then even if your exiled people are at the farthest horizon, I will gather them from there and bring them to the place I have chosen as a dwelling for my Name.'

[10]"They are your servants and your people, whom you redeemed by your great strength and your mighty hand. [11]Lord, let your ear be attentive to the prayer of this your servant and to the prayer of your servants who delight in revering your name. Give your servant success today by granting him favor in the presence of this man."

2 I went to Jerusalem, and after staying there three days ^{12}I set out during the night with a few others. I had not told anyone what my God had put in my heart to do for Jerusalem. There were no mounts with me except the one I was riding on.

^{13}By night I went out through the Valley Gate toward the Jackal Well and the Dung Gate, examining the walls of Jerusalem, which had been broken down, and its gates, which had been destroyed by fire. ^{14}Then I moved on toward the Fountain Gate and the King's Pool, but there was not enough room for my mount to get through; ^{15}so I went up the valley by night, examining the wall. Finally, I turned back and reentered through the Valley Gate. ^{16}The officials did not know where I had gone or what I was doing, because as yet I had said nothing to the Jews or the priests or nobles or officials or any others who would be doing the work.

^{17}Then I said to them, "You see the trouble we are in: Jerusalem lies in ruins, and its gates have been burned with fire. Come, let us rebuild the wall of Jerusalem, and we will no longer be in disgrace." ^{18}I also told them about the gracious hand of my God on me and what the king had said to me.

They replied, "Let us start rebuilding." So they began this good work.

Reflect

This passage is all about knowing *how* to help. Here, Nehemiah is saddened by the fact that the Israelites must return home to a ruined, broken and crumbling city, with walls that cannot protect them and houses that offer no shelter. By surveying the wreckage of Jerusalem carefully, Nehemiah is able to find a very practical way of helping the Israelites returning to their home from exile.

- **Question #1**: What actions do we see Nehemiah take in this passage?

- **Question #2**: Why do you think Nehemiah surveyed the city of Jerusalem before rebuilding it? What does Nehemiah do?

We must be attentive to the ROOTS of injustice. The only way we can understand injustice is to identify the underlying issues or problems that are creating it. Imagine there is a person in your community who is very angry and aggressive toward his children, often beating them for no reason. Our first reaction is to punish him for being violent, but if we just try to stamp out the problem of his anger we may be missing something and actually just escalating the tension. If we take some time to talk to this man and understand him, we may find out, for example, that he has a very difficult relationship with his wife. The best way to help him might be directing him to a good counselor so that he and his wife could talk to a wise and respected member of the community who could help them work out their disagreements.

When we witness injustice, we often have one of two reactions: we either feel so intimidated by the problem that we try to ignore it and forget about it, or we want to dive right in and do something straight away. But this passage from Nehemiah warns us against both. If we have the first reaction, nothing will change and injustice will grow. But if we have the second, we risk being ineffective or not actually addressing the root of the problem. When we take the time to understand the problems behind injustice and listen to someone who knows the situation better, we will be strong warriors of justice for God!

■ **Question #3:** What do you think we can learn about ourselves from observing injustice carefully?

Understanding injustice correctly leads to INNER change. In this passage, Nehemiah is clearly disturbed by the state of his people and he wants to do something about it. He then prays for wisdom and favor: "Lord, let your ear be attentive to the prayer of this your servant and to the prayer of your servants who delight in revering your name." Taking the time to ask for God's help and wisdom is not only wise, it is also a humbling experience.

When we have a correct understanding of why someone is suffering, we can better identify with them. And when we become more understanding of those who suffer injustice, we experience compassion for them. The word compassion means "to suffer with." In this way, our hearts start to become cleansed of the judgment or apathy we often feel toward those whose lives have been wrecked by injustice, making room for the love and mercy that is most effective in tackling injustice.

■ **Question #4:** Have you ever had the experience of suffering *with* someone? Jesus actually calls us to suffer with others. How does Nehemiah suffer *with* the Jews in Jerusalem in order to bring about justice?

In the 1990s, the city of Bogotá, Colombia, was in chaos. It was overrun with street gangs who would terrorize and rob the population, traffic was impenetrable, and the city was full of violence and lawlessness. The people either did not care about the laws or they lived in fear, knowing that the laws would not protect them.

Antanas Mockus, a mathematician and philosopher, ran for mayor in 1993 since he wanted to take on a new challenge. He had no experience, but he did have a discerning mind and a fresh perspective. Most importantly, he was known for being an honest man. While many leaders looked at the city and thought it needed a tough, strict hand to bring order, Mockus thought otherwise. He realized that the people no longer respected authority, so strictness would not work. Mockus knew he would have to take a different approach.

Instead of a heavy hand, Mockus used humor and art to influence the people of Bogotá. He would sometimes walk around the city in a spandex suit and cape and call himself Supercitizen. He hired 420 mime artists and clowns to stand in busy intersections of the city and conduct traffic. The clowns would poke fun at people who disobeyed traffic laws. They would walk behind people who were crossing the street illegally, copying them theatrically. People were not scared of the police, but they were scared of being made fun of in public!

Mockus also distributed "thumbs up" and "thumbs down" cards to people so that they could peacefully hold up signs in public when they saw citizens behaving well or badly. This was a successful program and led to a greater degree of public accountability. To highlight the seriousness of traffic accidents and the need to be aware of others on the road, he had big stars painted on the streets in places where pedestrians had been killed by drivers.

Mockus said of his rather eccentric methods, "In a society where human life has lost value, there cannot be another priority than re-establishing respect for life as the main right and duty of citizens." Since Mockus was elected in 1993, the homicide rate dropped from 80 per 100,000 inhabitants to 22 per 100,000 in 2003. During that time, deaths from traffic accidents dropped from an average of 1,300 per year to about 600.

"Saving a single life justifies the effort," he said.

Mayor Mockus took time to understand the problems his city faced before just leaping into his job. This led him to some very creative but effective ideas for helping restore justice to his city.[1]

💡 Review

What do you notice about the different parts of Nehemiah's prayer? How does this prayer help prepare him to do justice well?

❝❞ Respond

Is there an area of injustice in your community or within the systems of society that you do not entirely understand? How might you seek to understand the root of this issue? What are tangible actions you can take to learn more, understand the history, talk to people connected or survey the situation?

On your own or in a group, identify a current issue of injustice and brainstorm the various ways that different factors from many sectors have contributed to it.

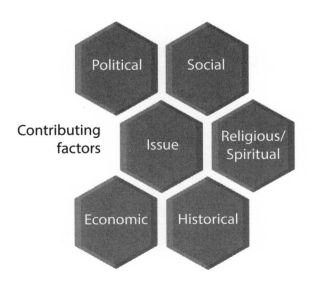

Mary, a widow in Uganda, rests against the door of her home, knowing she can live peacefully after IJM and local officials secured her land from those who tried to take it.

For Further Reflection

When all Israel heard the verdict the king had given, they held the king in awe, because they saw that he had wisdom from God to administer justice. (1 Kings 3:28)

I will listen to what God the LORD says;
   he promises peace to his people, his faithful servants—
   but let them not turn to folly. (Psalm 85:8)

Give me understanding, so that I may keep your law
   and obey it with all my heart. (Psalm 119:34)

12

The Voice of the Voiceless

In many parts of the world today the church is growing rapidly and is becoming a sizeable influence on society. Yet in so many other parts of the world the church is still a minority and, as such, feels quite disempowered. The fact that the church has traditionally stayed away from civic engagement has only added to this feeling of helplessness. This is typically either due to suspicion of governments and the world at-large, or perhaps due to the often erroneous interpretations of the Scriptures dealing with our roles and responsibilities in the world.

Through IJM's work in numerous countries around the world, we have come to realize that the church could in fact be quite an influence. In one East African country, local pastors of small congregations have begun to stand up to the rampant abuse of young girls in their communities—often at great risk to their lives—while in another they have begun to "adopt" victims of police abuse to care for them and to give voice to their families. In a Central American country, large denominations and Christian entities have begun to come together to stand as one united voice for victims of abuse and to rid their country of the scourge of sex abuse of little children. In several cities in South Asia, churches are coming together to form networks against human trafficking in order to advocate for the victims of abuse and to move the government to action.

We hope this session will give you an opportunity to reflect on what it would look like for you to be involved in the cause of the poor and the oppressed—to give voice to the voiceless. After all, you are God's chosen instrument in his divine plan to bring eternal shalom, and the simple fact is that you are required to reflect God's heart for justice. Know that you can make a difference.

Recall

During the last session we discussed our need to understand injustice so that we can respond in the best way. Was there ever a time when God asked you to respond to a person's need in a way that you did not understand? If so, what did you learn about God or about yourself? If not, what advice would you give to someone who felt like they were in that situation?

⌨ Read

Esther 3:1-14; 4:1-3; 4:9–5:8; 7:1-10

[1]After these events, King Xerxes honored Haman son of Hammedatha, the Agagite, elevating him and giving him a seat of honor higher than that of all the other nobles. [2]All the royal officials at the king's gate knelt down and paid honor to Haman, for the king had commanded this concerning him. But Mordecai would not kneel down or pay him honor.

[3]Then the royal officials at the king's gate asked Mordecai, "Why do you disobey the king's command?" [4]Day after day they spoke to him but he refused to comply. Therefore they told Haman about it to see whether Mordecai's behavior would be tolerated, for he had told them he was a Jew.

[5]When Haman saw that Mordecai would not kneel down or pay him honor, he was enraged. [6]Yet having learned who Mordecai's people were, he scorned the idea of killing only Mordecai. Instead Haman looked for a way to destroy all Mordecai's people, the Jews, throughout the whole kingdom of Xerxes.

[7]In the twelfth year of King Xerxes, in the first month, the month of Nisan, the *pur* (that is, the lot) was cast in the presence of Haman to select a day and month. And the lot fell on the twelfth month, the month of Adar.

[8]Then Haman said to King Xerxes, "There is a certain people dispersed among the peoples in all the provinces of your kingdom who keep themselves separate. Their customs are different from those of all other people, and they do not obey the king's laws; it is not in the king's best interest to tolerate them. [9]If it pleases the king, let a decree be issued to destroy them, and I will give ten thousand talents of silver to the king's administrators for the royal treasury."

[10]So the king took his signet ring from his finger and gave it to Haman son of Hammedatha, the Agagite, the enemy of the Jews. [11]"Keep the money," the king said to Haman, "and do with the people as you please."

[12]Then on the thirteenth day of the first month the royal secretaries were summoned. They wrote out in the script of each province and in the language of each people all Haman's orders to the king's satraps, the governors of the various provinces and the nobles of the various peoples. These were written in the name of King Xerxes himself and sealed with his own ring. [13]Dispatches were sent by couriers to all the king's provinces with the order to destroy, kill and annihilate all the Jews—young and old, women and children—on a single day, the thirteenth day of

the twelfth month, the month of Adar, and to plunder their goods. [14]A copy of the text of the edict was to be issued as law in every province and made known to the people of every nationality so they would be ready for that day.

4 When Mordecai learned of all that had been done, he tore his clothes, put on sackcloth and ashes, and went out into the city, wailing loudly and bitterly. [2]But he went only as far as the king's gate, because no one clothed in sackcloth was allowed to enter it. [3]In every province to which the edict and order of the king came, there was great mourning among the Jews, with fasting, weeping and wailing. Many lay in sackcloth and ashes.

[9]Hathak went back and reported to Esther what Mordecai had said. [10]Then she instructed him to say to Mordecai, [11]"All the king's officials and the people of the royal provinces know that for any man or woman who approaches the king in the inner court without being summoned the king has but one law: that they be put to death unless the king extends the gold scepter to them and spares their lives. But thirty days have passed since I was called to go to the king."

[12]When Esther's words were reported to Mordecai, [13]he sent back this answer: "Do not think that because you are in the king's house you alone of all the Jews will escape. [14]For if you remain silent at this time, relief and deliverance for the Jews will arise from another place, but you and your father's family will perish. And who knows but that you have come to your royal position for such a time as this?"

[15]Then Esther sent this reply to Mordecai: [16]"Go, gather together all the Jews who are in Susa, and fast for me. Do not eat or drink for three days, night or day. I and my attendants will fast as you do. When this is done, I will go to the king, even though it is against the law. And if I perish, I perish."

[17]So Mordecai went away and carried out all of Esther's instructions.

5 On the third day Esther put on her royal robes and stood in the inner court of the palace, in front of the king's hall. The king was sitting on his royal throne in the hall, facing the entrance. [2]When he saw Queen Esther standing in the court, he was pleased with her and held out to her the gold scepter that was in his hand. So Esther approached and touched the tip of the scepter.

[3]Then the king asked, "What is it, Queen Esther? What is your request? Even up to half the kingdom, it will be given you."

[4]"If it pleases the king," replied Esther, "let the king, together with Haman, come today to a banquet I have prepared for him."

[5]"Bring Haman at once," the king said, "so that we may do what Esther asks." So the king and Haman went to the banquet Esther had prepared. [6]As they were drinking wine, the king again asked Esther, "Now what is your petition? It will be given you. And what is your request? Even up to half the kingdom, it will be granted."

[7]Esther replied, "My petition and my request is this: [8]If the king regards me with

favor and if it pleases the king to grant my petition and fulfill my request, let the king and Haman come tomorrow to the banquet I will prepare for them. Then I will answer the king's question."

7 So the king and Haman went to Queen Esther's banquet, [2]and as they were drinking wine on the second day, the king again asked, "Queen Esther, what is your petition? It will be given you. What is your request? Even up to half the kingdom, it will be granted."

[3]Then Queen Esther answered, "If I have found favor with you, Your Majesty, and if it pleases you, grant me my life—this is my petition. And spare my people— this is my request. [4]For I and my people have been sold to be destroyed, killed and annihilated. If we had merely been sold as male and female slaves, I would have kept quiet, because no such distress would justify disturbing the king."

[5]King Xerxes asked Queen Esther, "Who is he? Where is he—the man who has dared to do such a thing?"

[6]Esther said, "An adversary and enemy! This vile Haman!"

Then Haman was terrified before the king and queen. [7]The king got up in a rage, left his wine and went out into the palace garden. But Haman, realizing that the king had already decided his fate, stayed behind to beg Queen Esther for his life.

[8]Just as the king returned from the palace garden to the banquet hall, Haman was falling on the couch where Esther was reclining.

The king exclaimed, "Will he even molest the queen while she is with me in the house?"

As soon as the word left the king's mouth, they covered Haman's face. [9]Then Harbona, one of the eunuchs attending the king, said, "A pole reaching to a height of fifty cubits stands by Haman's house. He had it set up for Mordecai, who spoke up to help the king."

The king said, "Impale him on it!" [10]So they impaled Haman on the pole he had set up for Mordecai. Then the king's fury subsided.

Reflect

■ **Question #1:** What do you think gave Esther the strength to go to King Xerxes, even though it may have cost her life?

When we step out in faith, God is WITH us. There are two places in this story where Esther shows faith and courage, and in both of those places God protects her and grants her incredible favor. First, she must go before the king even though she knows that unless the king is merciful, doing so carries a death sentence. But looking at the passage, we see that the king is not only merciful, but he is extremely generous to Esther. He says that he would even give her half of his kingdom if she asked! God blesses Esther's willingness to approach the king and demonstrates to Esther that he is with her.

The second place we see Esther's bravery is when she reveals to the king who she is and asks him to save her people. The king could have been furious—the Jews were an exiled people in Babylon, not fit to be kings and queens. Also, Esther asks very big things of the king—to take back an edict that had already been issued, making him look like a weak and indecisive ruler. But again, God protects Esther and blesses her. The king is not angry with her, but rather with Haman who enacted the edict.

It is interesting that the king's heart matches God's heart for his people in this passage. God is working all the time to rescue his people from injustice and death. He placed Esther in this prominent position for this purpose, but she still had to step out in faith. God also calls us to step out in faith and speak up for what concerns us, like Esther did. This is not always easy, but God will *always* be with us.

■ **Question #2:** Where do you see injustice in this story? Where do you see shalom breaking through?

Advocacy begins the process of restoring creation to SHALOM. When we are willing to advocate for or stand up and speak in defense of another person, God can use our words to end the injustice against that person. The end of this story shows just how powerful advocacy can be in bringing about justice. At the end of the story the perpetrator of injustice, Haman, is impaled on the gallows he had built to kill Mordecai. This is a very clear image of how God can turn injustice into justice and how God can restore shalom even to the most hopeless of situations.

Speaking up for people who are oppressed and sharing stories about injustice with your community is the first and crucial step in making a change. Nothing at all will change if others don't even *know* about injustice, so speaking up is incredibly important and incredibly effective.

■ **Question #3:** What was Mordecai's role in bringing justice? Why might it surprise someone reading this passage that God used Mordecai to bring his justice?

EVERYONE can be an advocate for justice. Think of Mordecai in this story. He was wearing sackcloth and sitting outside the city gates but he did not keep silent about the oppression of the Jews. And by speaking up he was able to influence someone who *did* have the power to influence the king. Incredibly, God places us in community so that when we start to speak about injustice, other people listen. God will often give our voices some influence so that others will hear and be educated about the issues of injustice.

Rusty Havens is a very sweet man from a small town in the state of Louisiana in the United States. Rusty works in a coffee shop. He is not an expert on issues of injustice and not at all what you would imagine of a justice advocate! But when Rusty found out about injustice and the work of IJM at a church conference, he said that a hole opened up in his heart. He had no idea that children were being sold as sex slaves or that families were having their land violently stolen from them every day. Rusty was so passionate and angry about this injustice that he knew he had to do something about it. He contacted IJM and asked them what he should do to help. They gave Rusty a stack of postcards and asked him to get them filled out. So every Sunday for a month, Rusty set up a small table at his church and told people about the injustice that was happening all over the world. Many people agreed to sign their names on postcards to send to their local state representatives, telling them that they were upset about injustice and asking the government to do something.

Rusty collected *thousands* of postcards just by telling people about injustice and asking them to sign their names. Rusty then sent those postcards to Louisiana's members of Congress, asking them to take action on a bill that would help the United States government lead the fight against human trafficking domestically and abroad. Previously, one of the senators had not been persuaded, telling Rusty that he would likely vote "no" on the bill. However, when this senator received the thousands of postcards that Rusty had collected—just by talking to his fellow church members, who told their friends, who told their friends—he responded to his constituents' request and decided to vote "yes" on the bill.

God used one ordinary man, just like you and me, with no experience to dramatically change his government's attitude to human trafficking.[1] The bill was eventually passed by the whole US government and the president, and the United States is now very involved in anti-trafficking around the world.

💡 Review

Besides speaking up, what else might be required of advocates for justice?

❝❞ Respond

Take some time to reflect on what you have learned. Look back at the statements you wrote in session one.

1. What assumptions did you make about God and justice that may not have been true?

2. Did you learn what you wanted to learn?

3. Were you able to answer your questions? Perhaps you have new questions! Record those here for further study:

Now consider the Scripture we've encountered together in this study.

An IJM staff member greets a boy in a community in India.

Early on, when Jesus' public ministry started to get messy, controversial and dangerous, Jesus asked his disciples if they wanted to leave. He knew that his disciples faced the choice that each of us face today: to walk with God closer to the oppressed and with brave hearts for love and justice, or to walk apart from God. Peter's response resonates deeply with us:

> "You do not want to leave too, do you?" Jesus asked the Twelve. Simon Peter answered him, "Lord, to whom shall we go? You have the words of eternal life. We have come to believe and to know that you are the Holy One of God." (John 6:67-69)

Consider the words of life that you've read throughout the Scriptures in this study. Identify three things that have impacted you. Then indicate your response. Let these thoughts move you to action with the God of justice.

His words of life	My response

A Closing Prayer:

> May God bless you with discomfort at easy answers, half-truths and superficial relationships so that you may live deep within your heart.
>
> May God bless you with anger at injustice, oppression and exploitation of people, so that you may work for justice, freedom and peace.
>
> May God bless you with tears to shed for those who suffer pain, rejection, hunger and war, so that you may reach out your hand to comfort them and to turn their pain to joy.
>
> And may God bless you with enough foolishness to believe that you can make a difference in the world, so that you can do what others claim cannot be done to bring justice and kindness to all our children and the poor. Amen

—A Franciscan Benediction

For Further Reflection

> Speak up for those who cannot speak for themselves,
>   for the rights of all who are destitute.
> Speak up and judge fairly;
>   defend the rights of the poor and needy. (Proverbs 31:8-9)

> Do not be overcome with evil, but overcome evil with good. (Romans 12:21)

Continue to remember those in prison as if you were together with them in prison, and those who are mistreated as if you yourselves were suffering. (Hebrews 13:3)

I swore never to be silent whenever and wherever human beings endure suffering and humiliation. We must always take sides. Neutrality helps the oppressor, never the victim. Silence encourages the tormentor, never the tormented. Sometimes we must interfere.
—Elie Wiesel

SOUTHEAST ASIA—CAMBODIA

MIEN'S STORY

Mien grew up in Svay Pak, a marginalized community in Cambodia that was notorious for selling very young girls for sex. Mien's family emigrated from Vietnam, and they were desperately poor. Her father spent what little money they earned on alcohol and her mother was helpless to stop his abuses.

Like many other girls growing up in the poor community, Mien was sold to a brothel one block from her own home when she was just fourteen years old. Night after night, Mien was sold to sex tourists and men who came to Svay Pak because they knew they could find young girls. The nightmare became a routine. Although she was minutes from her childhood home, Mien was trapped.

In 2003, IJM heard about Mien and the many other girls like her who were trapped and abused. IJM investigators assisted the Anti-Human Trafficking and Juvenile Protection Unit of the Cambodian National Police with its first-ever rescue operation. On that day, thirty-seven girls were rescued from sex slavery. The youngest girl was only five years old. But Mien hid from the police during the rescue operation. The owners had told her, time and time again, that if the police found her they would arrest her. Sadly, Mien was not rescued that day.

Her family moved north, to Siem Reap, near the popular tourist destination of Angkor Wat, a beautiful ancient temple. Mien was again sold to a brothel there where her life fell back into the same nightmare. Mien was sold night after night to men who paid to rape her. She said, "I despair—my life does not have meaning. . . . I feel like I don't want to do this anymore, but what else can I do? I have no skills and my family depends on the money I send to them every month."

But this would not be Mien's reality forever. IJM investigators started to gather evidence in the very same brothel where Mien was being exploited. The brothel was disguised as a massage parlor, but IJM soon documented evidence to reveal girls had been trafficked there to be sold for sex.

In 2007, IJM worked with an anti-trafficking unit of the police in Siem Reap to rescue women and girls who had been trafficked to a brothel,

Mien

including Mien and seven other girls, most of whom were minors. Mien was taken to a short-term aftercare shelter where she received crisis care and started a new life of freedom. IJM assisted the prosecutor to develop a strong legal case against the pimps and traffickers. At the end of the trial, justice was delivered: five perpetrators were convicted.

But Mien still had a lot of healing to do. In Cambodia, there is a proverb that says, "Men are like gold and women are like cloth." The meaning is that men can "dirty" themselves through sexual promiscuity then wash themselves off to shine like gold again. In contrast, a woman is believed to become "stained" forever, like a white cloth, tainted and worthless. That strong stigma, often leading to a feeling of worthlessness or loss of hope, is one of the greatest challenges for IJM aftercare teams.

Mien found an aftercare home where she felt safe and comfortable. The home is located in the very same community where Mien grew up. But the home has transformed the neighborhood—in fact, the very same brothel where Mien was first sold was bought by the aftercare home and turned into a community center for youth.

Mien began to thrive. She became a confident young woman and a mentor for others. She started to volunteer at the community youth center, reaching out to kids in the area—the very same neighborhood she had grown up in and the place where she was first exploited.

Today, Mien is married and lives with her husband; they are saving money in hopes of owning their own home someday. She sews beautiful silk pillow covers and other textiles, including uniforms for another micro-enterprise business. As Mien said, "Everything has changed."

Acknowledgments

This resource is the result of many people laboring faithfully in many different places over many years. We are truly grateful for your work. Particularly . . .

Thank you to the fantastic interns of IJM. Your energy and enthusiasm were huge gifts. Thank you for your research, writing and endless enthusiasm tracking down small details and stories: Matthew Robinson, Rosie Gillum, Erin Kattos, Elizabeth Williams, Blaire Bloxom, Lucy Harig and Kristin Schulz. Aaron Gaglia and Lilli Beard deserve particular mention—thank you for your extraordinary work!

Thank you to the fantastic people who work with churches and communities of faith. We are grateful for the ways that you lay down your lives so that others might know our God better. Thank you to all who participated in early versions of this curriculum and shared your experiences with us. Thank you, Miguel Lau—your pastor's heart and biblical insights are only surpassed by your passion for the global church!

Thank you to the Institute team. Larry Martin, thank you for your leadership and passion! Dave Healing, you provided the foundation upon which others built. Bethany, your leadership and passion continue to bless us. James Criss, thank you! To the brilliant Michael Thate, thank you. Jessica Kyle, you make things happen!

And a big thank you to Susan Conway—you carried us over the finish line. Your educator's heart, your global experience and your depth of insight combined in a special way on this project. Thank you, on behalf of all the students, past and present, who have been blessed by you and released to the work of justice through you.

What a privilege it is to work alongside you!

Bible Verses on Justice

Genesis 1:27

Genesis 12:3

Exodus 22:21-24

Leviticus 19:15

Deuteronomy 10:17-18

Deuteronomy 15:7-8

Deuteronomy 16:20

Nehemiah 9:27

Job 5:11-12;16

Job 31:16-22

Psalm 7:11

Psalm 9:9

Psalm 9:18

Psalm 10:17-18

Psalm 19:7-9

Psalm 30:11-12

Psalm 103:13

Proverbs 14:31

Proverbs 21:15

Isaiah 1:17

Isaiah 30:18

Isaiah 49:8-9

Isaiah 58:10-11

Isaiah 59:15-16

Jeremiah 21:12

Jeremiah 22:16

Ezekiel 34:16

Hosea 6:6

Amos 5:11

Amos 5:23-24

Micah 6:8

Zephaniah 3:19

Zechariah 11:7

Matthew 6:10

Matthew 6:19-20

Matthew 7:12

Matthew 15:32

Matthew 25:35-36

Luke 10:34

Luke 10:36-37

Luke 11:42

Luke 14:12-14

John 3:17

Romans 8:28

Romans 12:21

Galatians 3:28

Galatians 6:9

Philippians 2:3-4

Colossians 3:12

James 1:27

James 2:15-17

1 John 3:18

1 John 4:20

Revelation 21:4

For Further Reading on Justice and the Christian Life

Below is a list of books helpful for understanding the role of Christians in the work of justice and why we, as the body of Christ, should be engaged in it.

Byun, Eddie. *Justice Awakening: How You and Your Church Can Help End Human Trafficking*. Downers Grove, IL: InterVarsity Press, 2014.

Chester, Tim. *Justice, Mercy and Humility: The Papers of the Micah Network International Consultation on Integral Mission and the Poor*. Milton Keynes, UK: Paternoster, 2002.

Fuder, Dr. John, and Noel Castellanos, eds. *A Heart for the Community: New Models for Urban and Suburban Ministry*. Chicago: Moody Publishers, 2009.

Gonzalez, Justo. *Manana: Christian Theology from a Hispanic Perspective*. Nashville: Abingdon Press, 1990.

Haugen, Gary. *Good News About Injustice: A Witness of Courage in a Hurting World*. Downers Grove, IL: InterVarsity Press, 1999.

————. *Just Courage: God's Great Expedition for the Restless Christian*. Downers Grove, IL: InterVarsity Press, 2008.

Katongole, Emmanuel, and Chris Rice. *Reconciling All Things: A Christian Vision for Justice, Peace and Healing*. Downers Grove, IL: InterVarsity Press, 2008.

Keller, Timothy J. *Generous Justice: How God's Grace Makes Us Just*. New York: Riverhead Books, 2010.

Labberton, Mark. *The Dangerous Act of Loving Your Neighbor: Seeing Others Through the Eyes of Jesus*. Downers Grove, IL: InterVarsity Press, 2010.

Marshall, Chris. *The Little Book of Biblical Justice: A Fresh Approach to the Bible's Teachings on Justice*. Intercourse, PA: Good Books, 2005.

McNeil, Brenda Salter. *A Credible Witness: Reflections on Power, Evangelism and Race*. Downers Grove, IL: InterVarsity Press, 2008.

Perkins, John. *Let Justice Roll Down: John Perkins Tells His Own Story*. Grand Rapids: Baker, 2012.

————. *With Justice For All: A Strategy for Community Development.* Grand Rapids: Baker, 2011.

Wigg-Stevenson, Tyler. *The World Is Not Ours to Save: Finding the Freedom to Do Good.* Downers Grove, IL: InterVarsity Press, 2013.

Willard, Dallas. *The Divine Conspiracy: Recovering Our Hidden Life in God.* San Francisco: HarperSanFrancisco, 1998.

Wright, N. T. *Evil and the Justice of God.* Downers Grove, IL: InterVarsity Press, 2006.

Yoder, Perry. *Shalom: The Bible's Word for Salvation, Justice, and Peace.* Nappanee, IN: Evangel, 1987.

Facilitator's Guide

Your Role as a Group Facilitator:

- *Know your role*! Your job is to guide people through the discussion. You do not need to have all of the correct answers, and you don't need to be a teacher or trainer. This should be a place where people can learn and feel comfortable. Enjoy being with the group. The more prepared you are, the more confident you will feel. Begin each session with personal prayer, as you prepare to host the group, and then with group prayer. Use this opportunity to remind yourself and your group that this study is an opportunity to know the heart of God better. Invite him into the space and time of the group discussion.

- *Know your material*! Read through the material for the week at least a day in advance and identify the main theme of the session. A well-prepared group leader knows what is coming next and understands the material well before leading the discussion. This way you can manage your time well and answer any questions that may arise. You will also know when the discussion is getting off-track and if you need to steer it back in the right direction. Each session asks participants to *recall* what they've learned, to *read* and to *reflect* on the Scripture, to complete some type of exercise to assist with their learning, and to *respond* to the teaching through application to their daily lives and actions. Let these elements of the session be your guide and rely on the structure to help you facilitate.

- *Know your group*! Get to know the participants in your group. Write down and remember each of their names. Consider having a name plate for each person that you can use at every session. Make sure you allow time for introductions at the beginning of the first session and introduce yourself as well. It's helpful for you to build trust with the participants so that they'll share and learn comfortably.

- *Know your environment*! A good facilitator can help people learn in almost every environment. Make sure that each group member has the required materials and that the table and chairs are prepared. This way there will be more time for discussion and fewer distractions.

Leading Discussion Groups:

This is a discussion-based curriculum. Why is discussion so important to these sessions?

- People are more likely to remember what they have learned if they discuss it with another person.
- Discussion challenges people to consider other ideas so that people think about what they are learning.
- Discussion builds community among a group of learners.
- Discussion helps people feel comfortable asking questions.
- Discussion encourages participation and helps people stay focused on what they're learning.

Leading discussion groups is a great privilege, but it can be hard at times. You are responsible for making sure that the group gets to cover all the material in the allotted time, but this is not as easy as it sounds! You will have some people in your group who like to talk a lot and some people who are very shy. Sometimes the discussion may get off track or members of your group may get distracted. Here are some tips for leading a great discussion and making sure that everyone can not only participate but also contribute.

Encouraging Participation:

- Explain that you would like for everyone to participate. Tell participants that the goal is not to share the exact right answers but to discuss all of their ideas.
- Seat people in a circle or at tables so that they can see each other and have conversation. People are more likely to discuss ideas when they are facing other people and feel comfortable. You should sit in the group as well.
- Create some common expectations for the entire group. Here are a few that are helpful:
  - Everyone is encouraged to respect the opinions of other participants.
  - One person should be speaking at a time.
  - Answers should be concise so that multiple people can respond.
- Ask the group to take one minute to write down their answers first before you ask them to share. This allows them to think before answering.
- Call on people by name when they would like to share something.
- Don't be afraid to wait in silence while people are thinking. Sometimes people need to think before they are ready to share their ideas.

- Ask people to discuss briefly with the person next to them instead of with the whole group. This helps to give people some interaction and it causes everyone to participate in the discussion instead of having the same people share answers each time.

Managing Your Discussion Group:

You may encounter the following behavior types or personalities:

- **The chatterbox**: This person is always first to respond and wants to talk all the time. If you have someone like this in your group, it is a good idea to make sure that you start the discussion by letting someone else speak. As soon as you pose a question you can turn to a different member of the group and ask them to share first. Feel free to use a hand signal to tell people to wrap up what they are saying.

- **The shy bird**: This person may be extremely shy about talking. If this happens, you can ask a question directly to that person, such as, "(*Their name*), what do you think about this?" Make sure to be very encouraging to this person and thank them for sharing.

- **The distractor**: This person likes to start tangents and often leads the group off topic. Try not to cut people off, but feel free to use the hand signal to ask that person to wrap up and then pose a new question that brings the discussion back on track.

1: God the Creator

This week's discussion is focused around the story of creation and how the creation story gives us hearts for justice. The primary goal of this session is to make sure that discussion participants understand the main theme: **all people have inherent dignity and value** because they are made by God in his image. At the end of the session, participants are asked to respond by considering how they treat others and view themselves as God's image bearers. When we begin to understand that we each bear God's image, it impacts how we think, feel and behave, and challenges us to reflect God's character to those around us.

Key Points	Scripture Focus
• All people have dignity. • All people have inherent value, which is not dependent on anything they do, say or achieve. • God's creation reflects his goodness. • God creates human beings in his image. As image bearers, we must think about how we treat others. • God desires to have a relationship with each of us.	• Genesis 1:1-2, 11-12, 26-31; 2:1-3 • Psalm 139:13-16

2: Shalom and Human Responsibility

This week's discussion is focused around the idea of shalom, peace with justice, as God intended it. In John 10:10 Jesus says, "I have come that they may have life, and have it to the full." Shalom is life in its fullness, living in peace with God, others and with creation. It means that people are treated justly in relationships with each other. The vision of living in shalom can transform the way that we live toward a better future, with peace and justice for all. But in order to understand shalom, we must recognize that God has placed boundaries in our lives. These protect our relationships with God and with others. Boundaries allow us to thrive in shalom. This week's session will discuss **the role of boundaries in shalom, what healthy relationships look like in shalom and what healthy work looks like.**

Key Points	Scripture Focus
• God is intentional and sets things in place with particular order and specific purpose. • Shalom is peace. Beyond that, shalom is flourishing in the four key relationships in our lives: with God, with ourselves, with each other and with creation. • God creates boundaries, which are necessary for maintaining shalom. • When we keep these boundaries, we can thrive in healthy community and in work.	• Genesis 2:4-25

3: How Sin Corrupts Shalom

This week focuses on *how* sin enters humanity and corrupts shalom. We will look at the two main ways sin enters the world, how it turns shalom upside down and how it creates destruction in relationships. One type of sin, the sin of injustice, is particularly destructive and disregards the sanctity of human life. The main takeaway for this week's session is that **because of sin, shalom is corrupted and the world is not as it should be. Injustice is a particular type of sin that corrupts shalom.**

Key Points	Scripture Focus
• Sin comes through lies and deception and causes us to be self-focused. • Sin breaks down relationships with God and with one another. • When relationships with God and others are damaged by sin, shalom is broken. • The sin of injustice rejects the sanctity of life, violates others and forcefully takes shalom from them. • The sin of injustice is when one person uses his or her power to take the life and liberty away from another person.	• Genesis 3:1-13, 21-24; 4:1-12

4: Personal and Systemic Injustice

This session discusses injustice that happens as part of a system. A system is something larger than one individual; it is a combination of ideas, opinions, rules, processes, etc. Injustice is not just committed by individuals. It is committed by systems in society as well. These are injustices that are not as easily visible and therefore often go unnoticed because they are embedded in corrupt systems and processes. We read the story of Tamar in which a young, powerless and isolated girl takes a huge risk to expose the injustice of one of the most powerful men in society, the high priest Judah. This passage looks at the personal and systemic injustice against Tamar. The main takeaway for this session is that **as Christ-followers we must be thinking about personal injustice and systemic injustice, and how the systems and cultures around us promote injustice.**

Key Points	Scripture Focus
• Systems within society and culture can contribute to injustice. • Personal injustice happens because of the misuse of power and privilege, but systems can also disadvantage some people. • Injustice occurs when we forsake the law. • Injustice occurs when we deny individuals of their rights. • Injustice occurs when society fails to protect those who are vulnerable.	• Genesis 38:6-26

5: The Justice of God

The main theme of this session is that **God cares about justice.** We will look at this particularly in the story of God leading the Israelites out of slavery in Egypt, an event which was foundational for revealing to the Israelites who God is. It is important to note

Watch Grace's story at ijm.org/graces-story.

that this curricula is an introduction to injustice and suffering in the world. This session is not meant to address the deep theological implications for suffering. Try to focus the discussion on the issue of justice and what we can learn about this topic from the Scriptures.

Key Points	Scripture Focus
• God has a deep heart for justice. • God's justice involves punishment. • God brings justice through his people. • Through our human interaction to restore justice, relationships and communities are strengthened.	• Exodus 2:23–3:15; 12:29-36; 14:19-31

6: Jesus Messiah—New Creation

This week we look at the very start of Jesus' mission on earth. The Bible is clear that Jesus had diverse roles and intentions while here on earth. One of the things we see very clearly in Scripture and from Jesus' own description of his mission is that **a central purpose of Jesus' coming to earth was to do the work of justice,** just as God promised he would do way back in the Old Testament.

Key Points	Scripture Focus
• Jesus prioritizes the work of justice; he models this in his life on earth. • Jesus comes to restore shalom. • God is consistent and keeps his promises. • Jesus has come to bring real, tangible justice on earth.	• Isaiah 61:1-3 • Luke 4:1-21

7: Pictures of the Kingdom of God

This session looks at the life of Jesus and the kind of justice he displayed throughout his time here on earth. This is a discussion of some of the practical ways Jesus "did" justice and what we can learn about the kingdom of God from Jesus' actions. The main theme is that **Jesus' ministry was filled with the work of justice and he spent time with people in physical and spiritual need.**

Key Points	Scripture Focus
• In order to bring about justice, we must see people the way that God sees them. • Jesus chose to go against social norms to bring justice to those in need; we should too. • God will multiply our small efforts to build his kingdom through the work of justice.	• John 5:1-9 • Luke 14:1-6 • Matthew 14:13-21

8: Justice and the Cross of Christ

This week we look at the death of Jesus on the cross and what this means for us as we prepare to do the work of justice. We see that the cross reflects both justice and injustice. The main theme of this week is that **remembering Jesus' death on the cross gives us the tools and the strength we need to follow in his footsteps and do the work of justice.**

Key Points	Scripture Focus
• God restores shalom to a broken world through Jesus' death on the cross. • The cross assures us of God's heart for justice. • The cross of Christ gives us the *hope* we need to do the work of justice. • The cross of Christ gives us the *humility* we need to do the work of justice.	• Luke 23:13-49

9: The Church and Justice

This week's session focuses on the church's role in doing justice. These passages from Acts come just after Jesus ascended into heaven and left the disciples and the early Christians with the task of continuing the work that he started. In other words, the early church was to be Christ's hands and feet. **The early church and the apostles continued the work of justice and the work of evangelism as one and the same thing.** They were not separate in their eyes because they were not separate in Jesus' eyes. This is the main theme of the week: **we, as the church, are to continue the work of Christ.**

Key Points	Scripture Focus
• The work of evangelism and justice are carried out together. • The work of justice is carried out in our daily lives. • God multiplies our efforts and resources to do the work of justice in extraordinary ways. • God's power is required for us to do justice in our daily lives.	• Acts 2:42–3:10

10: Pleading for Justice

This session focuses on prayer and how important it is for bringing about justice and also being attuned to God's plan for justice. As Christ-followers, we should always be thinking about how we can do the work of justice on a daily basis. The main theme is that **prayer is a key component of the work of justice.** Encourage your group to pray for the work of justice.

Key Points	Scripture Focus
• Prayer is essential to the work of justice. • We need to pray faithfully and persistently. • Prayer teaches us to rely on God. • We need to pray with power. • We need to pray with humility.	• Luke 18:1-8 • Matthew 6:9-13

11: Surveying the Wreckage

The main theme of this session is that **we need to understand the injustice that we will face so we can persevere in doing the work of justice.** Having a correct understanding of injustice can be a transformative experience for us as individuals and helps us to be more effective in our work. It also helps us to find practical ways of doing justice. As we think about moving forward and addressing areas of injustice in our life and work, it is helpful to anticipate how we may react to injustice and what will help to strengthen us in our response.

Key Points	Scripture Focus
• We must understand the root causes of injustice so that we can persevere in our work to end it. • Understanding injustice correctly leads to inner change. • When we seek to understand injustice, it helps us to feel compassion for those who suffer.	• Nehemiah 1:1-11; 2:11-18

12: The Voice of the Voiceless

This week's session follows the story of Esther, which teaches us that **when we speak up about injustice in our communities, God can use us to do amazing things.** When we use the word "advocacy," we are referring to the ways that we can speak up for people, defend them and educate others about how they can

Watch Suhana's story at ijm.org/content/ray-hope.

help end the injustice. This is the last session in the curricula so participants are invited to reflect on what they have learned and how they will respond to God's invitation to seek justice.

Key Points	Scripture Focus
• When we step out in faith, God is with us and equips us. • God will often ask us to advocate for another person or people. • God uses our advocacy to restore shalom. • God can use all of us to end injustice, even the least likely person! Everyone can be an advocate.	• Esther 3:1-14; 4:1-3; 4:9–5:8; 7:1-10

Notes

1: God the Creator

[1]Jez Barnes, "Interview with Nicky and Pippa Gumbel," *The Month*, February 2013, 4, www
.st-stephens.org.uk/sites/st-stephens.org.uk/files/sst075_the_month_feb_2013_web.pdf.

2: Shalom and Human Responsibility

[1]Cornelius Plantinga Jr., as quoted by Amy Sherman in *Kingdom Calling* (Downers Grove, IL:
InterVarsity Press, 2011), 33-34 (www.calvin.edu/about/who-we-are/our-calling.htm).

[2]Nicholas Wolterstorff, "The Contours of Justice: An Ancient Call for Shalom," in *God and
the Victim*, ed. Lisa Barnes Lampman (Grand Rapids: Eerdmans and Neighbors Who Care,
1999), 113.

[3]Shukla Bose, "Teaching One Child at a Time," *TEDIndia*, 2009, ted.com/talks/shukla_bose_
teaching_one_child_at_a_time.html.

3: How Sin Corrupts Shalom

[1]"The Global Slavery Index," Walk Free Foundation, www.globalslaveryindex.org.

[2]"Vaneshawari's Story," *Loose Change to Loosen Chains: Students Freeing Modern Day Slaves Toolkit*,
International Justice Mission, www.ijm.org/sites/default/files/Loose-Change-Toolkit.pdf.

4: Personal and Systemic Injustice

[1]Tim Keller, "Tamar," Redeemer Presbyterian Church, December 2, 2001, http://sermons2
.redeemer.com/sermons/tamar.

[2]Niels Bohr, *The Political Arena (1934–1961)*, vol. 11 of *Niels Bohr: Collected Works*, ed. Finn
Aaserud (Amsterdam: Elsevier, 2005), 14.

5: The Justice of God

[1]"July 1 Rescue Brings Freedom to 47 Slaves from Single Brick Kiln," *International Justice
Mission*, July 10, 2009, www.ijm.org/news/july-1-rescue-brings-freedom-47-slaves-single
-brick-kiln.

6: Jesus Messiah—New Creation

[1]Orla Guerin, "Malala Yousafzai: Battling for an Education in Pakistan," *BBC News Asia*, July
11, 2013, bbc.co.uk/news/world-asia-23268708.

7: Pictures of the Kingdom of God

[1]Chris Hedges, "A Bosnian's Generosity Transcends the Conflict," *New York Times*, January 1, 1996, www.nytimes.com/1996/01/01/world/a-bosnian-s-generosity-transcends-the-conflict .html; see also The Rev. Tracey Carroll, "God's Favored Ones," St. Christopher's Episcopal Church, Chillicothe, OH, December 24, 2011, stchristophersfairborn.diosohio.org/dfc/news detail_2/3150918.

8: Justice and the Cross of Christ

[1]"St. Maximilian Kolbe," *Catholic-pages.com*, catholic-pages.com/saints/st_maximilian.asp.

9: The Church and Justice

[1]Jose Luis Gonzalez-Balado, *Stories of Mother Teresa: Her Smiles and Her Words* (Liguori Publications, May 1983).

10: Pleading for Justice

[1]John Calvin, *The Institutes of the Christian Religion*, ed. John T. McNeill, trans. Ford Lewis Battles, 2 vols. (Philadelphia: Westminster Press, 1960), 3.20.3.

[2]"Michael's Long Road to Freedom Finally Ends in a Kenyan Court," International Justice Mission, December 10, 2013, www.ijm.org/news/michael%E2%80%99s-long-road-freedom -finally-ends-kenyan-court.

11: Surveying the Wreckage

[1]Maria Cristina Caballero, "Academic Turns City into a Social Experiment," *Harvard University Gazette*, March 11, 2004, news.harvard.edu/gazette/2004/03.11/01-mockus.html.

12: The Voice of the Voiceless

[1]"Lake Charles Resident Stands Up Against Human Trafficking," 7KPLCtv.com, 2014 Worldnow and KPLC, www.kplctv.com/story/17759810/lake-charles-resident-stands-up-against-human -trafficking.

About the Authors

Abraham George is director of international church mobilization at International Justice Mission. He travels extensively to support IJM's field offices by leading conferences, facilitating pastoral training and connecting church leaders in the biblical work of justice.

Nikki A. Toyama-Szeto is senior director of the Institute for Biblical Justice at International Justice Mission in Washington, D.C. She provides strategic leadership to the Institute and to IJM's Global Prayer team, igniting passion for biblical justice throughout the global church. Previously she served as program director for InterVarsity's Urbana Student Missions Conference. She is the co-author of *Partnering with the Global Church* and *More Than Serving Tea*.

About International Justice Mission

International Justice Mission is a human rights agency that secures justice for victims of slavery, sexual exploitation and other forms of violent oppression. IJM lawyers, investigators and aftercare professionals work with local officials to secure immediate victim rescue and aftercare, to prosecute perpetrators, and to ensure that public justice systems—police, courts and laws—effectively protect the poor.

For more information visit ijm.org.

More Titles from InterVarsity Press and IJM

Good News About Injustice
978-0-8308-3710-6

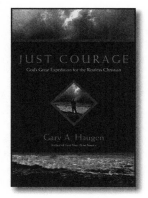

Just Courage
978-0-8308-3494-5

Deepening the Soul for Justice
978-0-8308-3463-1

For these and other titles, please visit ivpress.com.